Know Your Limits — *Then Ignore Them*

By

John Mason

101 "nuggets of truth" to help you break through barriers, reach new heights and live your dream!

EMBASSY BOOKS

Know Your Limits – *Then Ignore Them*

© 1999 John Mason

First Indian Edition : 2005

Published in India by :
EMBASSY BOOK DSITRIBUTORS,
120, Great Western Building,
Maharashtra Chamber of Commerce Lane,
Fort, Mumbai - 400 023. (India)
Tel : (022) 22819546 / 32967415
Email : embassy@vsnl.com

Cover Design by Banner Media Services, INC.

ISBN 10: 81-88452-24-6
ISBN 13: 978-81-88452-24-8

Printed and bound in India.

DEDICATION

To my beautiful wife, Linda, for her honesty and love.

To my daughter, Michelle, Dad's #1 fan.

To my son, Greg, for his help with so many things.

To my son, Mike, for being such an awesome giver.

To my son, Dave, for his contagious zest for life.

ACKNOWLEDGEMENTS

To Roger Bruhn, whose insight brings inspiration to me.

To Pastor Ed Gungor, who is teaching me to love God and celebrate people.

To Mike Loomis, for his unwavering support.

To Tim Redmond, for his gift of seeing the unseen.

To Tom Winters, for his godly counsel.

TABLE OF CONTENTS

INTRODUCTION

Have you ever seen an elephant waiting outside a tent at the circus? He stands there patiently, restrained by only a rope attached to a stake in the ground. Why doesn't the elephant just pull the stake up and run to freedom? Certainly he is strong enough to do so.

When the elephant is young, the stake holds him. In fact the elephant tries vigorously to free himself, chafing and cutting his leg in the process. He soon learns not to try and pull up the stake, and believes he can't the rest of his life. Aren't we a lot like that elephant? Are there things that are holding you back that really don't have the power to do so?

Limits are thrown at us every day. Each day we have a choice to accept or reject them. This book is written to attack limitations that hold you back from becoming all that you can be. I believe that each of us was made on purpose, for a purpose. And to reach that purpose we have to "pull up the stake" and run.

"MARCH OFF THE MAP."
(Joel Budd)

If you want to see if you can really swim, don't frustrate yourself with shallow water. Charles Schwab said, "When a man has put a limit on what he will do, he has put a limit on what he can do." Life is too short to think small.

Most people could do more than they think they can, but they usually do less than they think they can. You never know what you cannot do until you try. I agree with Oscar Wilde when he said, "Moderation is a fatal thing. Nothing succeeds like excess." Everything is possible–never use the word never.

Dr. J.A. Holmes said, "Never tell a young person that something cannot be done. God may have been waiting for centuries for somebody ignorant enough of the impossible to do that thing." If *you* devalue your dreams, no one else will raise the price. You will find that great leaders are rarely "realistic" by other people's standards.

The answer to your future lies outside the confines that you have right now. Cavett Robert said, "Any man who selects a goal in life which can be fully achieved has already defined his own limitations." Rather, as Art Sepulveda said, "Be a history maker and a world shaker." Go where you have never gone before.

When you climb the tallest tree, you capture the best fruit. Dag Hammarskjold said, "Is life so wretched? Is it rather your hands which are too small, your vision which is muddled? You are the one who must grow up." Gloria Swanson said, "Never say never. Never is a long, undependable thing, and life is too full of rich possibilities to have restrictions placed upon it."

To believe an idea impossible is to make it so. Consider how many fantastic projects have miscarried because of small thinking or have been strangled in their birth by a cowardly imagination. I like how Marabeau responded when he heard the word "impossible": "Never let me hear that foolish word again."

Pearl Buck said, "All things are possible until they are proved impossible—even the impossible may only be so as of now." Somebody is always doing what somebody else said couldn't be done. Dare to think unthinkable thoughts.

Develop an infinite capacity to ignore what others think can't be done. Don't just grow where you are planted. Bloom where you are planted and bear fruit. Daniel Webster said, "There is always room at the top." No one can predict to what heights you can soar. Even you will not know until you spread your wings.

Ronald McNair says, "You only become a winner if you are willing to walk over the edge." Take the lid off. Go out on a limb . . . that's where the fruit is! Spirella writes:

> There is no thrill in easy sailing when skies are clear and blue,
>
> There is no joy in merely doing things which any man can do.
>
> But there is some satisfaction that is mighty sweet to take,
>
> When you reach a destination that you thought you would never make.

NOTHING SIGNIFICANT WAS EVER ACCOMPLISHED BY A REALISTIC PERSON.

You can't test your destiny cautiously. "Don't play for safety–it's the most dangerous thing in the world," said Hugh Walpole. The key is this: forfeit the safety of what we are for what we could become. Unless you do something beyond what you have already done, you will never grow. Always pick an obstacle big enough to matter when you overcome it.

Conservative talk radio show host Rush Limbaugh has a great name for his outlandish tie collection–*No Boundaries*. What a great slogan to live our lives by. Get out of your comfort zone.

Know the rules, then break some. Take the limits off. Don't accept good enough as good enough. Tolerating mediocrity in others makes you more mediocre.

Melvin Evans said, "The men who build the future are those who know that greater things are yet to come, and that they themselves will help bring them about. Their minds are illumined by the blazing sun of hope. They never stop to doubt. They haven't the time." When you are a "realistic" person in everything you do, your focus is only on this immediate, measurable moment. Thinking this way limits you and restricts you in considering the unlimited possibilities of the future.

You can't make a place for yourself in the sun if you only live under the family tree. Go! Launch out! Be involved in something bigger than you. Do more!

Dorthea Brand stated, "All that is necessary to break the spell of inertia and frustration is this: act as if it were impossible to fail." An over–cautious person burns bridges of opportunity before he gets to them. Most of the people who sit around and wait for the harvest haven't planted anything. The average person doesn't want much and usually gets even less.

Until you give yourself to some great cause, you haven't really begun to fully live. "Security is mostly a superstition. It does not exist in nature, nor do the children of men as a whole experience it. Avoiding danger is no safer in the long run than outright exposure. Life is either a daring adventure, or nothing" (Helen Keller).

Nugget #3

IF YOU ARE ONLY LOOKING OUT FOR YOURSELF, LOOK OUT!

Is your favorite letter "I"? Listen: The cause of most of our problems is "I", no matter how we spell it. Change your favorite word from "I" to "You". The truth is, no one makes it on their own. George Adams said, "Everyone who has ever done a kind deed for us, or spoken one word of encouragement to us, has entered into the make-up of our character and of our thoughts, as well as our success."

Wesley Huber said, "There is nothing quite so dead as a self-centered man—a man who holds himself up as a self-made success, and measures himself by himself and is pleased with the result." Don't become a legend in your own mind.

Norman Vincent Peale observed, "The man who lives for himself is a failure. Even if he gains much wealth, power or position he is still a failure." Conceit makes us fools. The book of Proverbs reminds us, "Do you see a man wise in his own eyes? There is more hope for a fool than for him."

The man who believes in nothing but himself lives in a very small world. The best way to be happy is to forget yourself and focus on other people. Henry Courtney said, "The bigger a man's head gets, the easier it is to fill his shoes." The only reason pride lifts you up is to let you down. A swelled head always proves there is plenty of room for improvement. Even postage stamps become useless when they get stuck on themselves.

"The greatest magnifying glasses in the world are a man's own eyes when they look upon his own person" (Alexander Pope). Egotism is the only disease where the patient feels well while making everyone else around him feel sick. It blossoms but bears no fruit.

Those who sing their own praises seldom receive an encore. Charles Elliot intones, "Don't think too much of yourself. Try to cultivate the habit of thinking of others; this will reward you. Selfishness always brings its own revenge."

When you find yourself on a high horse, the best thing to do is to dismount at once. You can't push yourself forward by patting yourself on the back. Burton Hillis remarked, "It's fine to believe in ourselves, but we mustn't be too easily convinced." An egotist is his own best friend. I think that people who are deeply in love with themselves should get a divorce. The man who only works by himself and for himself is likely to be corrupted by the company he keeps.

I've observed that those who boast of being self-made usually have a few parts missing. You can recognize a self-made man; his head is oversized and his arms are long enough to pat himself on the back. A conceited person never gets anywhere because he thinks he has already "arrived." The higher you go in life, the more dependent you become on other people.

Work together with others. Remember the banana: everytime it leaves the bunch it gets peeled and eaten. Freckles would make a nice tan, if they would just get together. Few burdens are heavy when everyone lifts.

Nugget #4

THE MOST DANGEROUS PLACE TO BE IS IN THE MIDDLE OF THE ROAD.

My decision is maybe–and that's final!" Is this you? Have you ever noticed that some of the most miserable people in the world are those who can never make a decision? Being decisive is an absolute key to a successful life. Every accomplishment, great or small, starts with a decision. Nothing great was ever done without a decision.

If you commit yourself to being indecisive, what kind of life will you live? James Hightower says, "There's nothing in the middle of the road but yellow stripes and dead armadillos." The truth is that the most dangerous place to be is in the middle of the road.

Herbert Prochnow said, "There is a time when we must firmly choose the course which we will follow, or the relentless drift of events will make the decision for us." Being indecisive affects every area of our lives. The book of James says, "A double-minded man is unstable in all his ways." Too many people go through life not knowing what they want, but feeling sure they don't have it.

Don't be like a wheelbarrow, trailer or canoe. They need to be pushed, pulled or paddled to get anywhere. Realize that you're either moving other people to decisions or they're moving you. Edgar Roberts said, "Every human mind is a great slumbering power until awakened by a keen desire and a definite resolution to do." Decide to do something now to make *your* life better. The choice is yours.

David Ambrose remarked, "If you have the will to win, you have achieved half your success; if you don't, you have achieved half your failure." Lou Holtz said, "If you don't make a total commitment to whatever you are doing then you start looking to bail out the first time the boat starts leaking. It's tough enough getting the boat to shore with everybody rowing, let alone when a guy stands up and starts putting his life jacket on."

There is a difference between thinking and deciding. When you are thinking about something, you only do it when it is convenient. When you are decisive about something, you accept no excuses, only results. Lack of decisiveness has caused more failures than lack of intelligence or ability.

The moment you definitely decide, all sorts of things happen to help you that never would have otherwise occurred. There is no question that you create opportunities by being decisive. Lack opportunities? Make some decisions.

Maurice Witzer said, "You seldom get what you go after unless you know in advance what you want." Indecision often gives the advantage to the other person because they did their thinking beforehand. Helen Keller said, "Science may have found a cure for most evil, but it has found no remedy for the worst of them all–the apathy of human beings." Bertrand Russell said, "Nothing is so exhausting as indecision, and nothing is so futile."

Joseph Newton said, "Not what we have, but what we use, not what we see, but what we choose–these are things that mar or bless human happiness." Remain indecisive and you will never grow. To move from where you are, you must decide where you would rather be.

Nugget #5

WHEN YOUR CHANCES ARE SLIM AND NONE–GO WITH SLIM.

For many years, " 'Safety first' has been the saying of the human race . . . but it has never been the motto of leaders. A leader *must* face danger. He must take the risk, the blame and face the brunt of the storm" (Herbert Casson). If you want to be successful, you must either have a chance or take one. You can't get your head above water if you never stick your neck out.

Listen to Conrad Hilton: "I encourage boldness because the danger of seniority and pension plans tempt a young man to settle in a rut named security rather than find his own rainbow." Chuck Yeager remarked, "You don't concentrate on risk. You concentrate on results. No risk is too great to prevent the necessary job from getting done."

A dream that does not include risk is not really worthy of being called a dream. Halifax said, "The man who leaves nothing to chance will do few things badly, but he will do very few things." If you never take risks, you'll never accomplish great things. Everybody dies, but not everyone has lived.

Elizabeth Kenny reflected, "It is better to be a lion for a day than a sheep all your life." If you dare for nothing, you might as well hope for nothing. If you don't risk anything, you risk even more. John Newman wrote, "Calculation never made a hero." I agree with Lois Platford when she said, "You have all eternity to be cautious and then you're dead." Being destined for greatness requires you to take risks and confront great hazards.

It is an irrefutable fact that you will always miss 100% of the shots that you don't take. Morris West said, "If you spend your whole life inside waiting for the storms, you'll never enjoy the sunshine." No one reaches the top without daring.

Whenever you see a successful person, I guarantee that person took risks and made courageous decisions. Become known for doing what people said couldn't be done. Success always favors the gallant. David Mahoney said, "Refuse to join the cautious crowd that plays not to lose. Play to win."

Metastaisio observed, "Every noble acquisition is attended with its risk; he who fears to encounter the one must not expect to obtain the other." If you have found yourself throughout life never scared, embarrassed, disappointed or hurt it means you have never taken any risks.

You have an opportunity to improve yourself. If you want your life to get better, you'll have to take risks. There is simply no way you can grow without taking chances.

"ONE THOUGHT DRIVEN HOME IS BETTER THAN THREE LEFT ON BASE." (James Liter)

Ask yourself this question, "What am I really aiming at?" Delegate, simplify or eliminate low priorities as soon as possible. Do *more* by doing *less.* James Liter said, "One thought driven home is better than three left on base."

There are too many people in too many cars, in too much of a hurry, going too many directions, to get nowhere for nothing. "There is so little time for the discovery of all that we want to know about things that really interest us. We cannot afford to waste it on things that are only of casual concern for us, or in which we are interested only because other people have told us what we ought to be" (Alec Waugh). Without focus, there is no peace.

Follow this powerful advice from Paul the apostle who wrote, "This *one* thing I do . . . I press towards the mark." What you set your heart on will determine how you will spend your life. Carl Sandberg said, "There are people who want to be everywhere at once and they get nowhere."

How can you get what you want? William Locke answered, "I can tell how to get what you want; you've just got to keep a thing in view and go for it, and never let your eyes wander to the right or left or up or down. And looking back is fatal."

George Bernard Shaw wrote, "Give a man health and a course to steer, and he will never stop to trouble about whether he is happy or not." We know that Walt Disney was successful. Maybe the key to his success is found in his confession: "I love Mickey Mouse more than any women I've ever known." Now, that's focus!

Vic Braden said, "Losers have tons of variety. Champions take pride in just learning to hit the same old boring winners." Consider what George Robson said after winning the Indianapolis 500: "All I had to do was keep turning left."

If you chase two rabbits, both will escape. I believe you find happiness when you are going somewhere wholeheartedly, in one direction without regret or reservation. Do what you are doing while you are doing it. The more complicated you are, the more ineffective you will become.

Mark Twain said, "Behold the fool saith,'Put not all thine eggs in one basket'—which is but a manner of saying, 'Scatter your money and your attention.' But the wise man saith, 'Put all your eggs in one basket and—watch that basket.'" The quickest way to do many things is to do only one thing at a time. The only ones who will be remembered are those who have done one thing exceedingly well. Don't be like the man who said, "I'm focused, it's just on something else."

Nugget #7

IT IS BETTER TO BE ALONE THAN IN THE WRONG COMPANY.

Tell me who your best friends are, and I will tell you who you are. If you run with wolves you will learn how to howl. But, if you associate with eagles, you will learn how to soar to great heights. Proverbs says, "A mirror reflects a man's face, but what he is really like is shown by the kind of friends he chooses." The simple but true fact of life is that you become like those with whom you closely associate–for the good and the bad. Think about it; almost all of our sorrows spring out of relationships with the wrong people. Instead, "Keep out of the suction caused by those who drift backwards" (E. K. Piper).

The *less* you associate with some people, the *more* your life will improve. Any time you tolerate mediocrity in others it increases your mediocrity. A true Bulgarian proverb confirms, "If you find yourself taking two steps forward and one step backwards, invariably it's because you have mixed associations in your life." If a loafer isn't a nuisance to you, it's a sign that you are somewhat of a loafer yourself. I have discovered that an important attribute in successful people is their impatience with negative thinking and negative acting people.

A true friend is one who is there to care. They remain your friend even if you don't deserve to have a friend. They will see you through when others think that you're through.

Choose your associations carefully. This old saying is true: "He that lies down with dogs, shall rise up with fleas." Thomas Carlyle observed, "Show me the man you honor, and I will know what kind of man you are, for it shows me what your ideal of manhood is, what kind of man you long to be."

If you were to list your greatest benefits, resources or strengths, you would find that money is one of the least important ones while some of your greatest resources are the people you know. Mike Murdock said, "Someone is always observing you who is capable of greatly blessing you." A true friend sees beyond you to what you can be.

Invest in good relationships. The way to make a true friend is to be one. Your wealth is where your friends are. Consider what Francesco Guicciardini said: "Since there is nothing so well worth having as friends, never lose a chance to make the right ones."

As you grow, your associations will change. Some of your friends will not want you to go on. They will want you to stay where they are. Friends that don't help you climb, will want you to crawl. Your friends will stretch your vision or choke your dream. Those that don't increase you, will eventually decrease you.

Consider this: never receive counsel from unproductive people. Never discuss your problems with someone incapable of contributing to the solution, because those who never succeed themselves are always first to tell you how. Not everyone has a right to speak into your life. You are certain to get the worst of the bargain when you exchange ideas with the wrong person.

Don't follow anyone who's not going anywhere. With some people you spend an evening; with others you invest it. Be careful where you stop to inquire for directions along the road of life. Wise is the person who fortifies his life with the right friendships.

DARE TO BE WHAT YOU ARE.

Think about it: Aren't most of the discontented people you know trying to be something they are not or trying to do something they're not supposed to do? Resolve to be yourself. A Congolese proverb asserts, "Wood may remain ten years in the water, but it will never become a crocodile." The book of Jeremiah asks, "Can the Ethiopian change his skin or the leopard his spots?" Julius Hare advises, "Be what you are. This is the first step towards becoming better than you are."

"The curious paradox is that when I accept myself just as I am, then I can change" (Carl Rogers). Frederic Klopstock remarked, "He who has no opinion of his own, but depends on the opinions of others is a slave. To only dream of the person you are supposed to be is to waste the person you are." Nobody is so disappointed and so unhappy as the person who longs all of his life to be somebody other than who he really is.

The person who trims himself to suit everybody will soon whittle himself away. If you don't have a plan for your own life, you'll only become a part of someone else's. You can't carry two faces under one hat. Never wish to be anything but what you are. "It is better to be hated for what you are, than loved for what you are not" (Andre Gide).

"All good things which exist are the fruit of originality" (John Mills). There is only one life for you—your own. The person who walks in someone else's tracks never leaves his own footprints. Doris Mortman observed, "Until you make peace with who you are, you will never be content with what you have." Most of our challenges in life come from not knowing ourselves and ignoring our best, real virtues.

Most people live their entire lives as complete strangers to themselves. Don't let that happen to you. Leo Buscaglia counseled,

"The easiest thing to be in the world is you. The most difficult thing to be is what other people want you to be. Don't let them put you in that position." The opposite of courage is not fear. It is conformity. The most exhausting and frustrating thing in life is to live it trying to be someone else.

"My mother said to me, 'If you become a soldier you'll become a general, if you become a monk you'll end up as the pope.' Instead, I became a painter and wound up as Picasso," said the great artist. No one ever became great by imitation. Imitation is limitation. Don't be a copy of something. Make your own impression.

Nugget #9

DON'T END UP LIKE CONCRETE, ALL MIXED UP AND PERMANENTLY SET.

Change. Does this word scare or inspire you? Herbert Spencer said, "A living thing is distinguished from a dead thing by the multiplicity of the changes at any moment taking place in it." Change is evidence of life. It is impossible to grow without change. Those who cannot change their minds cannot change anything. The truth is, life is always at some turning point.

What people want is progress, if they can have it without change. Impossible! You must change and recognize that change is your greatest ally. The person who never changes his opinion, never corrects his mistakes. The fact is, the road to success is always under construction.

Yesterday's formula for success is often tomorrow's recipe for failure. The man who uses yesterday's methods in today's world probably won't be in business tomorrow. Consider what Thomas Watson, the founder of the IBM Corporation, said: "There is a world market for about 5 computers." Where would IBM be today if Mr. Watson had not been willing to change?

You cannot become what you are destined to be by remaining what you are. John Patterson said, "Only fools and dead men don't change their minds. Fools won't. Dead men can't." The same kind of thinking that has brought you to where you are today, will not necessarily take you where you want to go. Sante Boeve discovered this truth: "There are people whose watch stops at a certain hour and who remain permanently at that age."

Do not fear change; it is the unchangeable law of progress. Don't be a person whose mind is always open to new ideas, provided they are the same old ones. Defending your faults and errors only proves that you have no intention of quitting them. "There are people who not only strive to remain static themselves, but strive to keep everything else so . . . their position is almost laughably hopeless" (Odell Shepard).

Mignon McLaughlin said, "It's the most unhappy people who most fear change." When patterns and tradition are broken, new opportunities come together. All progress is due to those who were not satisfied to let well enough alone. They weren't afraid to change. Change is not your enemy—it is your friend.

Nugget #10

WOULD THE BOY YOU WERE BE PROUD OF THE MAN YOU ARE?

Living a double life will get you nowhere twice as fast. "Thoughts lead on to purposes; purposes go forth in action; actions form habits; habits decide character; and character fixes our destiny," said Tryon Edwards. Proverbs asserts, "A good name is rather to be chosen than great riches." Character is something you either have or are. Don't try to make something *for* yourself; instead, try to make something *of* yourself.

Character is the real foundation of all worthwhile success. A good question to ask yourself is, "What kind of world would this world be if everybody were just like me?" You are simply an open book telling the world about its author. John Morely remarked, "No man can climb out beyond the limitations of his own character."

Never be ashamed of doing right. Marcus Aurelius exhorted, "Never esteem as of advantage to thee that which shall make thee break thy word or lose thy self-respect." W. J. Dawson counseled, "You need not choose evil; but only to fail to choose good, and you drift fast enough towards evil." There is no such thing as a *necessary evil*. Phillip Brooks said, "A man who lives right and is right has more power in his silence than another has by his words."

Would your reputation recognize your character if they met in the dark? Desire what Psalms declared, "Create in me a pure heart, Oh Lord, and renew in me a right spirit." To change your character, you must begin at the control center–the heart. A bankruptcy of character is inevitable when you are no longer able to keep the interest paid on your moral obligations.

Henry Ward Beecher said, "No man can tell whether he is rich or poor by turning to his ledger. It is the heart that makes a man rich. He is rich according to what he is, not according to what he has." Live so that your friends can defend you, but never have to do so.

Consider what Woodrow Wilson said: "If you think about what you ought to do for people, your character will take care of itself." Excellence in character is shown by doing unwitnessed what we would be doing with the whole world watching.

You're called to grow like a tree, not like a mushroom. It's hard to climb high when your character is low. The world's best sermon is preached by the traffic sign: *Keep Right.*

Nugget #11

CRITICS THROW MUD, BUT LOSE GROUND.

The first and great commandment about critics is: *don't let them scare you*. No one can make you feel average without your permission. Charles Dodgson said, "If you limit your actions in life to things that nobody could possibly find fault with, you will not do much." Nothing significant has ever been accomplished without controversy or criticism.

When you allow other people's words to stop you, they will. To succeed in life you must overcome the many efforts of others to pull you down. Don't be afraid of what others say about you. Instead follow what Proverbs says, "Fear of man is a dangerous trap, but to trust in God means safety." If you think more about what other people think of you, you'll have more confidence in their opinion than you have in your own. Don't let your life depend on the permission and opinion of others.

Christopher Morley said, "The truth is, a critic is like a gong at a railroad crossing, clanging loudly and vainly as the train goes by." Many great ideas have been lost because those who had them couldn't stand the criticism and gave up. Know this: a critic is simply someone who finds fault without a search warrant. One of the easiest things to find is fault. "The most insignificant people are those most apt to sneer at others. They are safe from reprisals, and have no hope of rising in their own esteem but by lowering their neighbors" (William Hazlitt). Critics not only expect the worst, but make the worst of what happens.

When you make your mark in life, you always attract erasers. Dennis Wholey warned, "Expecting the world to treat you fairly because you are a good person is a little like expecting a bull not to attack you because you are a vegetarian." I agree with Fred Allen when he said, "If criticism had any real power to harm, the skunk would have been extinct by now." Great minds discuss ideas, good minds discuss events, small minds discuss other people.

You can't carve your way to success with cutting remarks. You will never move up if you are continually running someone down. I agree with Tillotson: "There is no readier way for a man to bring his own worth into question than by endeavoring to detract from the worth of other men." Henry Ford commented, "Men and automobiles are much alike. Some are right at home on an uphill pull; others run smoothly only going downgrade. When you hear one knocking all the time, it's a sure sign there is something wrong under the hood."

Remember this, if you are afraid of criticism, you will die doing nothing. If you want a place in the sun, you will have to expect some blisters and some sand kicked in your face. Criticism is a compliment when you know what you're doing is right.

Nugget #12

CLIMB OUT OF THE GRANDSTAND AND ONTO THE PLAYING FIELD.

You can't fulfill your destiny on a theory . . . it takes WORK. None of the secrets of success will work unless you do. You are made for action. Success simply takes good ideas and puts them to work. What the *free enterprise* system really means is that the more *enterprising* you are the more *free* you are. What we all need is less emphasis on *free* and more on *enterprise*.

Listen to Shakespeare: "Nothing can come of nothing." A belief is worthless unless converted into action. The Bible, a book of faith, talks about work over 500 times. Often, the simple answer to your problems is: *go to work.*

"Striving for success without hard work is like trying to harvest where you haven't planted" (David Bly). What you believe doesn't amount to very much unless it causes you to wake up from your dream and start working. You cannot just dream yourself into what you could be. The only time a lazy person ever succeeds is when he tries to do nothing. A famous old saying says it best: "Laziness travels so slowly, poverty soon overtakes it."

When you are lazy, you must work twice. It is always a trying time for the person who is always trying to get something for nothing. Did you notice? We weren't given apple juice, we were given apples. Some say *nothing* is impossible, yet there are a lot of people doing *nothing* every day.

Some do things while others sit around becoming experts on how things might be done. The world is divided into people who do things and people who talk about doing things. Belong to the first group–there is far less competition.

"All men are alike in their promises. It is only in their deeds that they differ" (Moliere). Wishing has never made a poor man wealthy. Robert Half nails it: "Laziness is the secret ingredient that goes into failure, but it's only kept a secret from the person who fails."

Tell yourself: "Inspirations never go in for long engagements; they demand immediate marriage to action" (Brendon Francis). If the truth were known, most of our troubles arise from loafing when we should be working, and talking when we should be listening.

There is a man in the world who never gets turned down, wherever he chances to stray;

He gets the glad hand in the populous town, or out where the farmers make hay;

He is greeted with pleasure on deserts of sand, and deep in the isles of the woods;

Wherever he goes there is a welcoming hand–he's the man who delivers the goods.

(Walt Whitman)

Nugget #13

IF YOU FIND AN EXCUSE, DON'T PICK IT UP.

When it comes to excuses, the world is full of great inventors. Don't spend half your life telling what you are going to do and the other half explaining why you didn't do it. An alibi is the proof that you did do what you didn't do, so that others will think you didn't do what you did.

Mistakes have hidden powers to help us, but they fail in their mission of helping us when we blame them on other people. When you use excuses you give up your power to change and improve. So, "Never mind whom you praise, but be careful whom you blame" (Edmond Gosse). You can fall down many times, but you won't be a failure until you say that someone else pushed you.

Failures are experts at making excuses. There are always enough excuses available if you are weak enough to use them. The world simply does not have enough crutches for all the lame excuses. It's always easier to find excuses instead of time for the things we don't want to do.

So, find a way, not an excuse. There is no excuse for being full of excuses. When you make a mistake and then make an excuse for it, you have made two mistakes. Note this truth: "The fox condemns the trap, not himself" (Blake). Don't find yourself talking like that old fox!

Never complain and never explain. "Admitting errors clears the score and proves you wiser than before" (Arthur Guiterman). Doing a job right is always easier than fabricating an alibi for why you didn't. You waste time and creative energies thinking up excuses.

An excuse is a foundation used to build a house of failure. An alibi is worse and more troubling than a lie, because an alibi is a lie with other lies attached to it. It's been said that an excuse is a thin skin of falsehood stretched tightly over a bald–faced lie.

Nearly all failures come from people who have the habit of making excuses. When you're good at making excuses, it's hard to excel at anything else. The book of Proverbs says, "Work brings profit; talk brings poverty." Don't make excuses, make progress.

There may be many reasons for failure, but not a single excuse. Never let a challenge become an alibi. You have a choice: you can let the obstacle be an alibi or an opportunity. No alibi will ever support your purpose in life.

The person who really wants to do something finds a way; the other finds an excuse. Success is a matter of luck; just ask any failure. Don't buy that alibi.

Nugget #14

IT'S NOT THE MOUNTAIN WE CONQUER, BUT OURSELVES.

If you would like to know who is responsible for most of your troubles, take a look in the mirror. If you could kick the person responsible for most of your problems, you wouldn't be able to sit down for three weeks. It's time for us to stay out of our own way.

Louis XIV commented, "There is little that can withstand a man who can conquer himself." "Our business in life is not to get ahead of others, but to get ahead of ourselves–to break our own records, to outstrip our yesterdays by today, to do our work with more force than ever before" (Stewart Johnson).

Ralph Waldo Emerson said, "It is impossible for man to be cheated by anyone but himself." "Our best friends and our worst enemies are the thoughts we have about ourselves"(Dr. Frank Crane). Proverbs declares, "As a man thinks, so is he, and as a man chooses, so is he." Norman Vincent Peale remarked, "Do not build up obstacles in your imagination."

Stop looking only at where you are and start looking at what you can be. Be careful of where your mind wanders; your words and actions follow it. It's followed by words at any moment and actions very soon.

No one can defeat you unless you first defeat yourself. Self-image sets the boundaries and limits of each of our individual accomplishments. Charles Colton said, "We are sure to be losers when we quarrel with ourselves; it is civil war." If you doubt yourself, listen to Alexander Dumas: "A person who doubts himself is like a man who enlists in the ranks of his enemy and bears arms against himself." Tim Redmond observed, "Don't commit treason against your own life and purpose."

You carry with you the world in which you must live. Know this: when you have a great dream, your mind will be your biggest enemy. Facing major obstacles in life? James Allen answered, "You are the handicap you must face. You are the one who must choose your place." Remember you are your own doctor when it comes to curing cold feet, a hot head and a stuffy attitude.

"Your future depends on many things, but mostly on you" (Frank Tyger). You may succeed if nobody else believes in you, but you will never succeed if you don't believe in yourself. Zig Ziglar observes, "What you picture in your mind, your mind will go to work to accomplish. When you change your pictures you automatically change your performance." Whatever you attach consistently to the words "I am", you will become.

Nugget #15

ENVY SHOOTS AT OTHERS AND WOUNDS ITSELF.

Envy is the most unproductive of ideas. There is no single advantage to be gained from it. If you compare what you want with what others have, you will be unhappy. Instead, be thankful for what you have and you'll discover happiness.

It's not trying to "keep up with the Jones'" that causes so much trouble. It's trying to pass them. Washington Allston reflected, "The only competition worthy of a wise mind is within himself." Nothing gets you further behind than trying to keep up with people who are already there.

If envy were a disease, everyone would be sick. Frances Bacon said, "Envy has no holidays. It has no rest." The envy that compares us to others is foolish and very unproductive.

What makes us discontented with our personal condition is the absurd belief that others are so much happier that we are. You'll find it's hard to be happier than others if you believe others to be happier than they are. Think about it; do you *really* know how happy they are? Thomas Fuller said, "Comparison, more than reality, makes men happy or wretched."

Helen Keller said, "Instead of comparing our lot with those who are more fortunate than we are, we should compare it with the lot of the great majority of our fellow men. It then appears that we are among the privileged." It's time to say "Thanks" not "Why me?"

Richard Evans said, "May we never let the things we can't have or don't have, spoil our enjoyment of the things we do have and can have." The book of Proverbs says, "A relaxed attitude lengthens a man's life; jealousy rots it away." St. John Chrysostom reflected, "As a moth gnaws a garment, so doeth envy consume a man."

Envy provides the mud that failure throws at success. There are many roads to an unsuccessful life, but envy is the shortest of them all.

Nugget #16

YOU'RE EITHER A THERMOMETER OR A THERMOSTAT.

Several years ago I met with a friend who I have known for over ten years. He looked at me and said, "John, I see all the great things that are happening in your life and how you are increasing in so many different ways. But, as I began to look at *your* life I became full of doubt as to what was happening in *my* life." He said, "It caused me to doubt myself because I had not had the same success that you have."

I turned, looked at him and said, "Well, if it's true that you feel bad because I've been successful, then would it be true that you would feel better if I had had terrible failures and had been doing much worse over the past several years?"

He gave me a quizzical look and responded, "No, that would not be true."

I replied, "Well, if it is true for one it is true for the other. Really, it shows how inaccurate your thinking is. What happens in my life has nothing to do with what is happening in your life."

You will find that successful peoples' main concern is rarely what others are thinking. I believe that God rarely uses a person whose main concern is what others are thinking. In fact, judging and comparing yourself to others is a major waste of time. This thinking halts progress and inhibits your forward motion.

Never measure your success by what others have or haven't done. It's never fair to compare. You're either a voice or an echo. I agree with Pat Riley when he said, "Don't let other people tell you what you want." "Don't take anybody else's definition of success as your own" (Jacqueline Briskin).

No one can build a personal destiny upon the faith or experience of another person. You have to do your own growing, no matter how tall your dad is.

31

Your faults will never vanish by calling attention to the faults of others. Many people have the mistaken idea that they can make themselves great by showing how small someone else is. It isn't necessary to blow out the other person's light to let your light shine brighter.

If you think you are doing better than the average person, you're an average person. Why would you want to compare yourself with someone average? Too many people seem to know how to live everybody's life but their own. We need to stop comparing ourselves to others.

BETTER IS BETTER.

The time is always right to do the right thing. "Be driven by excellence. To be driven by excellence so at the end of each day, each month, each year, and indeed at the end of life itself we must ask one important question: have we demanded enough of ourselves, and by our example, inspired those around us to put forth their best effort and achieve their greatest potential?" (Richard Huseman).

More harm has been done by weak people than by wicked people. Most of the problems of this world have been caused by the weakness of good rather than by the strength of evil.

The true measure of a person is in his height of ideals, the breadth of his sympathy, the depth of his convictions, and the length of his patience. Consider what the book of James says: "Therefore, to one who knows the right thing to do, and does not do it, to him it is sin."

"Of all the paths a man could strike onto, there is, at any given moment, a best path . . . a thing which, here and now, if it were of all things wisest for him to do . . . to find this path and walk in it" (Thomas Carlyle). The right train of thought will take you to a better station in life. Eddie Rickenbacker encouraged us to "Think positively and masterfully, with confidence and faith, and life becomes more secure, more fraught with action, richer in achievement and experience."

If you want greatness, then forget greatness and earnestly pursue what is right. Then you can find both. Coach John Wooden said, "Success is peace of mind, which is a direct result of knowing you did your best to become the best that you are capable of being." Harold Taylor said, "The roots of true achievement lie in the will to become the best that you can become." Elevate your personal standards of quality. Whatever you thought was good enough for now, add 10% more. Stand for what's right, then you win, even if you "lose."

The biggest mistake you can make in life is not to be true to the best you know. George Bernard Shaw remarked, "Keep yourself clean and bright; you are the window through which you must see the world." Follow Ralph Sockman's advice: "Give the best that you have to the highest you know—and do it now."

Nugget #18

WHEN YOU MAKE MISTAKES, LEARN FROM THEM AND DON'T RESPOND WITH ENCORES.

Paul Galvin at the age of thirty-three had failed twice in business. He attended an auction of his own storage battery business. With his last $750, he bought back the battery eliminator portion of it. That part became Motorola. Upon his retirement in the 1960's, he said, "Do not fear mistakes. You will know failure. Continue to reach out." George Bernard Shaw said, "A life spent making mistakes is more useful than a life spent doing nothing." To expect your life to be perfectly tailored to your specifications is to live a life of continual frustration.

David McNally mused, "The mistake–riddled life is much richer, more interesting, and more stimulating than the life that has never risked or taken a stand on anything." What is the difference between champions and the average person? Tom Hopkins says, "The single most important difference between champion achievers and average people is their ability to handle rejection and failure." Listen to S. I. Hayakawa: "Notice the difference between what happens when a man says to himself, 'I failed three times,' than what happens when he says, 'I am a failure.'" Failure is a situation, never a person.

You can't travel the road to success without a puncture or two. Mistakes are often the best teachers. The book of Ecclesiastes advises, "In the day of prosperity be joyful, but in the day of adversity consider." Oswald Avery advises, "Whenever you fall, pick something up." The man who invented the eraser had the human race pretty well figured out. You will find that people who never make mistakes never make anything else. It's true: you can profit from your mistakes. That's why I'm convinced I'll be a millionaire.

Failure is not falling down, but staying down. Be like Jonah, who when swallowed by a large fish, proved that you can't keep a good man down. Remember a stumble is not a fall. In fact, a stumble may prevent a fall. Herman Melville wrote, "He who has never failed somewhere, that man cannot be great."

Not remembered for his failures but for his successes, inventor Thomas Edison reflected, "People are not remembered by how few times they failed, but by how often they succeed." Every wrong step can be another step forward. David Burns said, "Assert your right to make a few mistakes. If people can't accept your imperfection, that's their fault."

Louis Boone said, "Don't fear failure so much that you refuse to try new things. The saddest summary of life contains three descriptions, could have, might have, and should have." Robert Schuller wrote, "Look at what you have left, never look at what you have lost." If you learn from them, mistakes are very valuable. Cultivate this attitude and you will never be ashamed to try.

The person who never makes a mistake takes orders from someone who does. Frederick Robertson related, "No man ever progressed to greatness and goodness but through great mistakes." William Ward said, "Failure is delay, but not defeat. It is a temporary detour, not a dead end street."

Nugget #19

"WORRY GIVES A SMALL THING A BIG SHADOW."
(Swedish Proverb)

The great evangelist Billy Sunday once said, "Fear knocked at my door. Faith answered . . . and there was no one there." Now that's the proper response to fear. Fears, like babies, grow larger by nursing them. Disraeli says, "Nothing in life is more remarkable than the unnecessary anxiety which we endure, and generally create ourselves." We must act in spite of fear . . . not because of it. If you are afraid to step up to the plate, you will never hit a home run.

Lucy Montgomery said, "It only seems as if you are doing something when you are worrying." Worry doesn't help tomorrow's troubles, but it does ruin today's happiness. "A day of worry is more exhausting than a day of work" (John Lubbock).

When you worry about the future, there will soon be no future for you to worry about. No matter how much a person dreads the future, he usually wants to be around to see it. Unfortunately, more people worry about the future than prepare for it.

Never trouble trouble until trouble troubles you. Arthur Roche said, "Worry is a thin stream of fear trickling through the mind. If encouraged, it cuts a channel into which all other thoughts are drained."

Sister Mary Tricky said, "Fear is faith that it won't work out." Instead, do what the book of I Peter says, "Let him (God) have all your worries and cares, for he is always thinking about you and watching everything that concerns you."

Dr. Rob Gilbert advised, "It's all right to have butterflies in your stomach. Just get them to fly in formation."

Fear holds you back from flexing your risk muscle. So, consider this: what you fear about tomorrow is not here yet. George Porter said, "Always be on guard against your imagination. How many lions it creates in our paths, and so easily! And we suffer so much if we do not turn a deaf ear to its tales and suggestions."

Worry is like a dark room, because dark rooms are where negatives are developed. If you can't help worrying, remember worrying can't help you either. Worry never fixes anything. Shakespeare wrote, "Our doubts are traitors, and they make us lose what we oft might win, by fearing to attempt." Emanuel Celler says, "Don't roll up your pant legs before you get to the stream."

"If you are distressed by anything external, the pain is not due to the thing itself, but to your estimate of it and this you have the power to revoke at any moment" (Marcus Aurelius). Fear can keep you from going where you could have won. Don't let your fears steal from you and prevent you from pursuing your dream. Most people believe their doubts and doubt their beliefs. So, do like the old saying and "feed your faith and watch your doubts starve to death." Worry is a route that leads from somewhere to nowhere; never let it direct your life.

Nugget #20

SMILE OFTEN AND GIVE YOUR FROWN A REST.

There is a facelift you can perform yourself that is guaranteed to improve your appearance. It's called a smile. Laughter is like changing a baby's diaper–it solves a problem and makes things more acceptable for awhile. Cheer up. A dentist is the only person who is supposed to look down in the mouth. Robert Frost said, "Happiness makes up in height for what it lacks in length." Abraham Lincoln said, "Most folks are about as happy as they make up their minds to be." The worst day that you can have is the day you have not laughed.

The optimist laughs to forget. The pessimist forgets to laugh. You might as well laugh at yourself once in awhile–everyone else does. The only medicine that needs no prescription, has no unpleasant taste, and costs no money, is laughter.

A smile is a curve that you throw at another and always results in a hit. A smile goes a long way, but you're the one that must start it on its journey. Your world will look brighter from behind a smile. He who laughs, lasts.

Henry Ward Beecher said, "A person without a sense of humor is like a wagon without springs–jolted by every pebble on the road." Take to heart the words of Mosche Wadocks: "A sense of humor can help you overlook the unattractive, tolerate the unpleasant, cope with the unexpected, and smile through the unbearable." Your day goes the way the corners of your mouth turn.

I believe that every time you smile, and even much more so when you laugh, you add something to your life. A smile is a curve that helps us see things straight. Janet Layne said, "Of all the things you wear, your expression is the most important."

Proverbs says, "A merry heart doeth good like a medicine." A good laugh is the best medicine, whether you are sick or not.

"The world is like a mirror; frown at it, and it frowns at you. Smile and it smiles too" (Herbert Samuel). Every man who expects to receive happiness is obligated to give happiness. Cheerfulness is contagious, but it seems like some folks have been vaccinated against the "infection." The trouble with being a grouch is that you have to make new friends every month.

The wheels of progress are not turned by cranks. Tom Walsh says, "Every minute your mouth is turned down you lose 60 seconds of happiness." Paul Bourge wrote, "Unhappiness indicates wrong thinking, just as ill health indicates a bad regime." It's impossible to smile on the outside without feeling better on the inside. If you can laugh at it, you can live with it.

It was only a sunny smile,

But it scattered the night.

Thus little it cost in giving,

It made the day worth living.

(Anonymous)

Nugget #21

ENTHUSIASM MOVES THE WORLD.

" Think excitement, talk excitement, act out excitement, and you will become an excited person. Life will take on a new zest, with deeper interests and greater meaning. You can talk, think, and act yourself into enthusiasm or dullness and into monotony or into unhappiness. By the same process you can build up inspiration, excitement and a surging depth of joy" (Norman Vincent Peale). You can succeed at almost anything for which you have limitless enthusiasm. The world belongs to the enthusiastic.

A major difference between people is their level of enthusiasm. Your enthusiasm reflects your reserves, your unexploited resources and perhaps your future. Winston Churchill said, "Success is going from failure to failure without loss of enthusiasm." You will never rise to great heights without joy and enthusiasm.

"No one keeps up his enthusiasm automatically" (Papyrus). Enthusiasm must be nourished with new actions, new aspirations, new efforts and new vision. It's your own fault if your enthusiasm is gone. You have failed to feed it. What's enthusiasm? Henry Chester answers, "Enthusiasm is nothing more or less than faith in action." Helen Keller said, "Optimism is the faith that leads to achievement." Nothing can be done without hope or confidence.

It isn't our position, but our disposition that makes us happy. Remember, some people freeze in the winter. Others ski. A positive attitude always creates positive results. Attitude is a little thing that makes a big difference. Depression, gloom, pessimism, despair and discouragement stop more people than all illnesses combined.

You can't deliver the goods if your heart is heavier than the load. "We act as though comfort and luxury were the chief requirements of life, when all that we need to make us really happy is something to be enthusiastic about" (Charles Kingsley). Count your blessings; don't think your blessings don't count.

There is a direct correlation between our passion and our potential. You could be the light of the world, but no one will know it unless the switch is turned on. Follow what the book of Ecclesiastes says, "Whatever your hand finds to do, do it with all your might." Being positive is essential to achievement and the foundation of true progress.

If you live a life of negativity you will find yourself seasick during your entire voyage. The person who is negative is half–defeated before even beginning.

I agree with Winston Churchill when he said, "I am an optimist. It does not seem too much use being anything else." Have you ever noticed that no matter how many worries a pessimist has, he always has room for one more? Remember the Chinese proverb: "It is better to light a candle than to curse the darkness." Das Energi said, "Vote with your life. Vote yes!"

Nugget #22

NO OBSTACLE WILL EVER LEAVE YOU THE WAY IT FOUND YOU.

"Times of general calamity and confusion have ever been productive of the greatest minds. The purest ore is produced from the hottest furnace, and the brightest thunderbolt is the one elicited from the darkest storm" (Caleb Colton). The door to opportunity swings on the hinges of adversity. Problems are the price of progress. The obstacles of life are intended to make us better, not bitter. Adversity has advantages.

Obstacles are merely a call to strengthen, not quit. Ann Giminez says, "Between you and anything significant will be giants in your path." You cannot bring about change without confrontation. The truth is, if you like things easy, you will have difficulties. If you like problems, you will succeed. The biggest successes are the ones who solve the biggest problems.

If you have a dream without problems you don't really have a dream. Have the attitude of Louisa May Alcott: "I am not afraid of storms for I am learning how to sail my ship." Samuel Lover said, "Circumstances are the rulers of the weak; but they are the instruments of the wise." Don't let your problems take the lead. You take the lead. The problem you face is simply an opportunity for you to do your best.

The Chinese have this proverb that says, "The gem cannot be polished without friction, nor man perfected without trials." It seems that great trials are the necessary preparation for greatness. Consider what Jesus said: "Here on earth you will have many trials and sorrows; but cheer up, for I have overcome the world."

What attitude do we need to have toward difficulties? William Boetcker said, "The difficulties and struggles of today are but the best price we must pay for the accomplishment and victory of tomorrow." Lou Holtz advised, "Adversity is another way to measure the greatness of individuals. I never had a crisis that didn't make me stronger."

When you encounter obstacles, you will discover things about yourself that you never really knew. You will also find out what you really believe. Every problem introduces a person to himself.

Challenges make you stretch—they make you go beyond the norm. Martin Luther King, Jr. said, "The ultimate measure of man is not where he stands in moments of comfort and convenience, but where he stands at times of challenge and controversy." Turning an obstacle to your advantage is the first step towards victory.

Life is as uncertain as a grapefruit's squirt. Consider what Sydney Harris said, "When I hear somebody say that 'Life is hard', I am always tempted to ask, 'Compared to what?'" We might as well face our problems. We can't run fast or far enough to get away from them all. Rather, we should have the attitude of Stan Musial, the famous Hall of Fame baseball player. Commenting on how to handle a spit ball, he said, "I'll just hit the dry side of the ball." Charles Kettering said, "No one would have crossed the ocean if he could of gotten off the ship in the storm." The breakfast of champions is not cereal, it's obstacles.

A SHADY PERSON NEVER PRODUCES A BRIGHT LIFE.

There is no limit to the height you can attain by remaining on the level. Honesty is still the best policy. However, today it seems there are less policyholders than there used to be. George Braque said, "Truth exists, only falsehood has to be invented." Cervantes said, "Truth will rise above falsehood as oil above water."

White lies leave black marks on your reputation. You can't stretch the truth without making your story look pretty thin. When you stretch the truth, it snaps back at you.

Truth will win every argument if you stick with it long enough. Though honesty may not be popular, it is always right. The fact that nobody wants to believe what's true, doesn't keep it from being true.

Two half-truths don't make a whole truth. In fact, beware of half-truths. You may have gotten a hold of the wrong half. You will find that a lie has no legs. It has to be supported by other lies. T.L. Osborn says, "Always tell the truth and you never have to remember what you said."

The truth is one thing for which there are no known substitutes. There is no acceptable substitute for honesty. There is no valid excuse for dishonesty.

Nothing shows dirt like a white lie. It may seem that a lie may take care of the present, but it has no future. Hope built on a lie is always the beginning of loss.

Herbert Casson said, "Show me a liar and I will show you a thief." A lie's main assignment is to steal from you and others. George Bernard Shaw said, "The liar's punishment is not in the least that he is not believed, but that he cannot believe anyone else."

Liars have no true friends. How can you trust them? "If you lie and then tell the truth, the truth will be considered a lie" (Sumerian). A liar will not be believed even if they tell the truth. An honest person alters their ideas to fit the truth and a dishonest person alters the truth to fit their ideas.

There are no degrees of honesty. The only way to be free is to be a person of truth. Truth is strong and it will prevail. There is no power on earth more overpowering than the truth. Consider what Pearl Buck said: "Truth is always exciting. Speak it, then. Life is dull without it."

Nugget #24

PERSISTENT PEOPLE BEGIN THEIR SUCCESS WHERE MOST OTHERS QUIT.

Do you want to accomplish something in life? Be like the stone cutter. Jacob Riis says, "Look at the stone cutter hammering away at the rock, perhaps a 100 times without as much as a crack showing in it. Yet at the 101st blow it will split in two and I know it was not the last blow that did it, but all that had gone before." Whatever you want to accomplish in life will require persistence. Champion race car driver Rick Mears says, "To finish first you must first finish."

All things come to those who persistently go after them. Perseverance is the result of a strong will. Stubbornness is the result of a strong won't. Montesquieu said, "Success often depends on knowing how long it will take to succeed." The secret of success is: never let down and never let up. Consider what Proverbs says: "Seest thou a man diligent in his business? he shall stand before kings."

Many times success consists of hanging on one minute longer. Calvin Coolidge said, " 'Press on' has solved and always will solve the problems of the human race." You will find that persistent people always have this attitude: they never lose the game, they just run out of time. Compte de Buffon says, "Hold on; hold fast; hold out. Patience is genius."

Joel Hause said, "You may be whatever you resolve to be. Determine to be something in the world and you will be something. 'I cannot' never accomplished anything; 'I will try' has wrought wonders." Herbert Caufman adds, "Spurts don't count. The final score makes no mention of a splendid start if the finish proves that you were 'an also ran'."

Keep in mind the words of Hamilton Holt: "Nothing worthwhile comes easily. Half effort does not produce half results. It produces no results. Work, continuous work and hard work is the only way to accomplish results that last." No one finds life worth living. You must make it worth living.

Ralph Waldo Emerson said, "The great majority of men are bundles of beginnings." I agree with Charles Kettering when he said, "Keep on going and the chances are you will stumble on something perhaps when you are least expecting it." Be like the bulldog: "The nose of the bulldog is slanted backwards so he can continue to breathe without letting go" (Winston Churchill).

Persistence prevails when all else fails. The truth is that persistence is a bitter plant, but it has sweet fruit. Joseph Ross said, "It takes time to succeed because success is merely the natural reward of taking time to do anything well." Persistence is the quality that is most needed when it is exhausted. Victory always comes to the most persevering.

IF YOU WAIT TOO LONG, THE FUTURE IS GONE BEFORE YOU GET THERE.

Ask yourself: "If I don't take action now, what will this ultimately cost me?" When a procrastinator has finally made up his mind, the opportunity has always passed by. Edwin Markum writes:

When duty comes a knocking at your gate,

Welcome him in; for if you bid him wait,

He will depart only to come once more

And bring seven other duties to your door.

What you put off until tomorrow, you'll probably put off tomorrow, too. Success comes to the man who does today what others were thinking of doing tomorrow. The lazier a man is, the more he is going to do tomorrow. According to William Halsey, "All problems become smaller if you don't dodge them, but confront them. Touch a thistle timidly, and it pricks you; grasp it boldly, and its spines crumble."

Wasting time wastes your life. Cervantes pondered, "By the street of By and By, one arrives at the house of never." The procrastinator doesn't go through life–they're pushed through it. "The wise man does at once what the fool does finally" (Gracian).

"Someday" is not a day of the week. Doing nothing is the most tiresome job in the world. When you won't start, your difficulties won't stop. Tackle any difficulty now–the longer you wait the bigger it grows. Procrastinators never have small problems because they always wait until their problems grow up.

In the game of life nothing is less important than the score at half time. "The tragedy of life is not that man loses, but that he almost wins" (Haywood Broun). Don't leave before the victory happens! Robert Lewis Stevenson commented, "Saints are sinners who kept on going." The race is not always to the swift, but to those who keep on running.

Most people who sit around waiting for their ship to come in find it is a *hard*ship. The things that come to a person who waits seldom turn out to be the things they've waited for. The hardest work in the world is that which should have been done yesterday. Hard work is usually an accumulation of easy things that should have been done last week.

Sir Josiah Stamp said, "It is easy to dodge our responsibilities, but we cannot dodge the consequences of dodging our responsibilities." William James reflected, "Nothing is so fatiguing as the eternal hanging on of an uncompleted task." The book of Ecclesiastes says, "If you wait for perfect conditions, you'll never get anything done." Jimmy Lyons said, "Tomorrow is the only day in the year that appeals to a lazy man."

"A man with nothing to do does far more strenuous 'labor' than any other form of work. But my greatest pity is for the man who dodges a job he knows he should do. He is a shirker, and boy! What punishment he takes . . . from himself" (E.R. Collcord). Carve out a future; don't just whittle away the time.

"THE PURPOSE OF LIFE IS TO HAVE A LIFE OF PURPOSE."
(Robert Byrne)

A re you stumbling toward an uncertain future? You can predict your future by the awareness you have of your unique purpose. Too many people know what they are running from, but not what they are running to. First, concentrate on finding your purpose, then concentrate on fulfilling it. Having a powerful *why* will provide you with the necessary *how*. Purpose, not money, can be your strongest asset.

Myles Monroe said, "There is something for you to start that is destined for you to finish." Take care of your purpose and the end will take care of itself. When you base your life on principle, 99% of your decisions are already made. Considering an action? Listen to Marcus Aurelius: "Without a purpose nothing should be done."

"The height of your accomplishments will equal the depth of your convictions. Seek happiness for its own sake, and you will not find it; seek for purpose and happiness will follow as a shadow comes with the sunshine" (William Scolavino). As you reach for your destiny it will be like a magnet that pulls you, not like a brass ring that only goes around once. Destiny draws.

John Foster said, "It is a poor disgraceful thing not to be able to reply, with some degree of certainty, to the simple questions, 'What will you be? What will you do?" Dr. Charles Garfield added, "Peak performers are people who are committed to a compelling mission. It is very clear that they care deeply about what they do and their efforts, energies and enthusiasms are traceable back to that particular mission." You're not truly free until you've been made captive by your mission in life.

William Cowper said, "The only true happiness comes from squandering ourselves for a purpose." Note Proverbs when it says, "Whatever your plan is just know that nothing else will satisfy you."

Don't part company with your future. It is an anchor in the storm. A purposeless life is an early death. What you believe about your mission in life is the force that determines what you accomplish or fail to accomplish in life.

The average person's life consists of 20 years of having their parents ask where he or she is going, 40 years of having a spouse ask the same question and at the end, the mourners wondering the same thing. Martin Luther King, Jr. said, "If a man hasn't discovered something that he will die for, he isn't fit to live." Abandon yourself to destiny.

Nugget #27

DON'T EVER STart YOUR DAY IN NEUTRAL.

Seize the moment! Opportunities are coming to you or by you every day. Today was once the future from which you expected so much in the past. Horatio Dresser said, "The ideal never comes. Today is ideal for him who makes it so." Live for today. Don't let what you have within your grasp today be lost entirely because only the future intrigued you and the past disheartened you.

Doing the best at this moment puts you in the best place for the next moment. When can you live if not now? All the flowers of tomorrow are in the seeds of today. Seneca said, "Begin at once to live." Ellen Metcalf remarked, "There are many people who are at the right place at the right time but don't know it." It is okay to take time to plan, but when the time of action has arrived, stop thinking and go for it!

Marie Edgeworth said, "There is no moment like the present. The man who will not execute his resolutions when they are fresh on him can have no hope from them afterwards; for they will be dissipated, lost, and perished in the hurry and scurry of the world, or sunk in the slough of indolence."

John Burroughs said, "The lesson which life repeats and constantly reinforces is, 'Look under foot.' You are always nearer than you think . . . The great opportunity is where you are. Do not despise your own place and hour." The most important thing in our lives is what we are doing now.

Know the real value of today. I agree with Jonathan Swift when he said, "May you live all the days of your life." The future that you long and dream for begins today. Ralph Waldo Emerson said, "Write it on your heart that every day is the best day of the year."

The regrets that most people experience in life come from failing to act when having an opportunity. Albert Dunning said, "Great opportunities come to all, but many do not know that they have met them. The only preparation to take advantage of them is . . . to watch what each day brings."

I agree with Martial when he said, "Tomorrow life is too late; live today." Wayne Dyer observed, "Now is all we have. Everything that has ever happened, anything that is ever going to happen to you, is just a thought." Today, well lived, will prepare you for both the opportunities and obstacles of tomorrow.

Noah didn't wait for his ship to come in—he built one. Few know when to rise to the occasion. Most only know when to sit down. Many spend too much time dreaming of the future, never realizing that a little of it arrives every day. I agree with Ruth Schabacker when she said, "Every day comes bearing its own gifts. Untie the ribbons."

Nugget #28

EVERYBODY NEEDS HELP FROM SOMEBODY.

Serving others is one of life's most awesome privileges. Albert Schweitzer said, "The only ones among you who will really be happy are those who have sought and found how to serve." Pierre de Chartin commented, "The most satisfying thing in life is to have been able to give a large part of oneself to others." Follow the counsel of Carl Reilland: "In about the same degree as you are helpful you will be happy."

Hunt for the good points in people. Remember they have to do the same in your case. Then do something to help them. If you want to get ahead, be a bridge not a wall. Love others more than they deserve. Dr. Frank Crane said, "The golden rule is of no use unless you realize that it is your move." Each human being presents us with an opportunity to serve.

John Andrew Holmes said, "The entire population of the universe, with one trifling exception, is composed of others." Too often we expect everyone else to practice the golden rule. The golden rule may be old, but it hasn't been used enough to show any signs of wear. We make a first class mistake if we treat others as second class people.

You can't help others without helping yourself. Kindness is one of the most difficult things to give away since it usually comes back to you. The person who sows seeds of kindness enjoys a perpetual harvest. I agree with Henry Drummond when he said, "I wonder why it is that we are not kinder to each other . . . how much the world needs it! How easily it is done!"

Do you want to get along better with others? Be a little kinder than necessary. A good way to forget your own troubles is to help others out of theirs. When you share, you do not lessen, but increase your life.

Theodore Spear said, "You can never expect too much of yourself in the matter of giving yourself to others." The taller a bamboo grows, the lower it bends. Martin Luther King, Jr. said, "Everybody can be great . . . because anybody can serve."

True leadership begins with servanthood. Harry Fosdick said, "One of the most amazing things ever said on earth is Jesus' statement, 'He that is greatest among you shall be your servant.' None have one chance in a billion of being thought of as really great a century after they're gone except those who have been servants of all."

Henry Burton wrote:

> Have you had a kindness shown?
>
> Pass it on!
>
> Twas not given for thee alone,
>
> Pass it on!
>
> Let it travel down the years,
>
> Let it wipe another's tears,
>
> Till in heaven the deed appears
>
> Pass it on!

Nugget #29

SMALL STEPS ARE A BIG IDEA.

Success comes from daring to take small steps. After being faithful in small steps, you'll look back and be able to say, "I'm still not where I want to be, but I'm not where I was." Julia Carney said, "Little drops of water, little grains of sand, make the mighty ocean and the pleasant land." Author Louis L'Amour wrote, "Victory is won not in miles but in inches. Win a little now, hold your ground and later win a lot more." Sometimes we're given a little, in order to see what we will do with a lot.

Dale Carnegie said, "Don't be afraid to give your best to what seemingly are small jobs. Every time you conquer one it makes you that much stronger. If you do the little jobs well, the big ones will tend to take care of themselves." Your future comes one hour at a time. Thomas Huxley observed, "The rung of a ladder was never meant to rest upon, but to enable a man to put his other foot higher."

Never be discouraged when you make progress, no matter how slow or small. Be only wary of standing still. A success is a person who does what they can with what they have, where they are. Helen Keller said, "I long to accomplish a great and noble task but it is my chief duty to accomplish small tasks as if they were great and noble."

"Nobody makes the greater mistake than he who did nothing because he could only do a little" (Edmond Burke). Small deeds done are better than great deeds planned. I believe that you should care just as much about the small things in your life as the big things. Why? Because, if you are faithful in the small things, the big things will take care of themselves.

The prize of successfully completing one duty is the opportunity to do another. R. Smith said, "Most of the critical things in life, which become the starting points of human destiny, are little things." Do little things now and big things will come to you asking to be done.

One thing is certain: what isn't tried won't work. The most important thing is to begin, even though the first step is the hardest. I agree with Vince Lombardi: "Inches make champions." Take one small step right now. Don't ignore the small things. The kite flies because of its tail. It's the little things that count: sometimes a safety pin carries more responsibility than a bank president.

H. Storey remarked, "Have confidence that if you have done a *little* thing well, you could do a *bigger* thing well, too." Consider what Pat Robertson said: "Despise not the day of small beginnings because you can make all your mistakes anonymously." Value the little things. One day you may look back and realize they were the big things. Dante said, "From a little spark may burst a mighty flame." Remember this on your way up; the biggest dog was once a pup.

Nugget #30

START WHERE YOU ARE.

Start with what you have, not with what you don't have. Opportunity is always where you are, never where you were. To get anywhere you must launch out for somewhere or you will get nowhere.

Hamilton Mabie said, "The question for each man to settle is not what he would do if he had the means, time, influence and education advantages, but what he will do with the things he has." Each of us has an ability to begin to create what we need from something that is already here.

Everyone tends to underrate or overrate that which they do not possess. Ed Howe said, "People are always neglecting something they can do and trying to do something they can't do."

I agree with Teddy Roosevelt when he said, "Do what you can, with what you have, where you are." The only way to learn anything thoroughly is by starting at the bottom (except when learning how to swim). To be successful, do what you can.

Ken Keys, Jr. said, "To be upset over what you don't have is to waste what you do have." The truth is that many are successful because they didn't have the advantages others had.

Epicurus said, "Do not spoil what you have by desiring what you have not; but remember that what you now have was once among the things only hoped for." Henri Amiel observed, "Almost everything comes from almost nothing."

No improvement is so certain as that which proceeds from the right and timely use of what you already have. Everyone who has arrived had to begin where they were.

The truth is, you can't know what you can do until you try. The most important catalyst to reaching your dream is starting right where you are. Edward Hail said, "I cannot do everything, but I still can do something; and because I cannot do everything, I will not refuse to do the something I can do."

No longer forward nor behind

I look in hope or fear;

But, grateful, take the good I find,

The best of now and here.

(John Greenleaf Whittier)

BE . . .

Be . . . yourself.

Be . . . positive.

Be . . . thankful.

Be . . . decisive.

Be . . . merciful.

Be . . . persistent.

Be . . . honest.

Be . . . excellent.

Be . . . confident.

Be . . . patient.

Be . . . faithful.

Be . . . committed.

Be . . . dedicated.

Be . . . focused.

Be . . . forgiving.

Be . . . enthusiastic.

Be . . . hopeful.

Be . . . trustworthy.

Be . . . loyal.

Be . . . helpful.

Be . . . kind.

Be . . . happy.

Be . . . courageous.

Be . . . generous.

Be . . . loving.

Be . . . dependable.

Be . . . wise.

Be . . . pure.

Be . . . obedient.

Be . . . purposeful.

Be . . . effective.

Be . . . creative.

Be . . . responsible.

Be . . . devoted.

Be . . . patient.

Be . . . optimistic.

Be . . . compassionate.

COUNT YOUR BLESSINGS AND YOU'LL ALWAYS SHOW A PROFIT.

Do you count your blessings or think your blessings don't count? Do you have an attitude of gratitude? When you stop to think more, you'll stop to thank more. Of all our feelings, gratitude seems to have the shortest memory.

Cicero said, "A thankful heart is not only the greatest virtue, but the parent of all other virtues." The degree that you are thankful is a sure gauge of your spiritual health.

To lose, you don't have to have anything stolen from you; all you have to do is take everything you have for granted. Instead, when you count all your blessings, you will always show a profit.

Today, replace regret with gratitude. Be grateful for what you have, not sorry for what you have not. If you can't be thankful for what you have, then be thankful for what you have escaped.

Henry Ward Beecher said, "The unthankful . . . discovers no mercies; but the thankful heart . . . will find in every hour, some heavenly blessings." The more you complain, the less you'll obtain.

"If we get everything we want, we will soon want nothing that we get" (Vernon Luchies). If you don't enjoy what you have, how could you be happier with more?

The seeds of discouragement will not grow in a thankful heart. Erich Fromm remarked, "Greed is a bottomless pit which exhausts the person in an endless effort to satisfy the need without ever reaching satisfaction."

Epicurus reflected, "Nothing is enough for the man to whom enough is too little." It's a sure sign of mediocrity to be moderate with our thanks. Don't find yourself so busy asking others for favors that you have no time left to thank them. I relate to what Joel Budd said: "I feel like I'm the one who wrote *Amazing Grace*."

"Happiness always looks small while you hold it in your hands, but let it go, and you learn at once how big and precious it is" (Maxim Gorky). I believe we should have the attitude of George Hubert, when he said, "Thou O Lord hast given so much to me, give me one more thing—a grateful heart." Don't find yourself at the end of your life saying, "What a wonderful life I've had! I only wish I'd appreciated and realized it sooner."

> Thank God for dirty dishes;
>
> they have a tale to tell.
>
> While other folks go hungry,
>
> we're eating pretty well.
>
> With home, and health, and happiness,
>
> we shouldn't want to fuss;
>
> For by this stack of evidence,
>
> God's very good to us.

Nugget #33

IF YOU LOOK BACK TOO MUCH, YOU'LL SOON BE HEADING THAT DIRECTION.

There is no future in the past. Mike Murdock said, "Stop looking at where you have been and start looking at where you can be." Your destiny is always forward, never backward. Katherine Mansfield advised, "Make it a rule of life never to regret and never to look back. Regret is an appalling waste of energy. You can't build on it. It's only good for wallowing in."

A farmer once said his mule was awfully backward about going forward–this is also true of many people today. Are you backward about going forward? You are more likely to make mistakes when you act only on past experiences. Phillip Raskin said, "The man who wastes today lamenting yesterday will waste tomorrow lamenting today." Squash the "good old days" bug.

The past is always going to be the way it was. Stop trying to change it. Your future contains more happiness than any past you can remember. Rosy thoughts about the future can't exist when your mind is full of the blues about the past. Believe that the best is yet to come.

Oscar Wilde said, "No man is rich enough to buy back his past." Consider what W. R. Ing said: "Events in the past may be roughly divided into those which probably never happened and those which do not matter." The more you look back, the less you will get ahead. Thomas Jefferson was right when he said, "I like the dreams of the future better than the history of the past." Many a "has-been" lives on the reputation of their reputation.

Hubert Humphrey mused, "The good old days were never that good, believe me. The good new days are today, and better days are coming tomorrow. Our greatest songs are still unsung." If you find yourself depressed, it's usually because you are living in the past. What's a sure sign of stagnation in your life? When you dwell on the past at the expense of the future.

I agree with Laura Palmer's advice: "Don't waste today regretting yesterday instead of making a memory for tomorrow." David McNally said, "Your past cannot be changed, but you can change your tomorrow by your actions today." Never let yesterday use up too much of today. The book of Proverbs says, "The wise man looks ahead. The fool attempts to fool himself and won't face the facts." It's true what Satchel Paige said: "Don't look back. Something may be gaining on you."

"Living in the past is a dull and lonely business; looking back strains the neck muscles, causing you to bump into people not going your way" (Edna Ferber). The first rule for happiness is: avoid lengthy thinking on the past. Nothing is as far away as one hour ago. Charles Kettering added, "You can't have a better tomorrow if you are thinking about yesterday all the time." Your past doesn't equal your future.

WHAT BENEFIT IS RUNNING IF YOU'RE ON THE WRONG ROAD?

Beverly Sills says, "There are no shortcuts to any place worth going." The way to the top is neither swift nor easy. Nothing worthwhile ever happens in a hurry–so be patient. Because of impatience, we are driven too soon from what we're supposed to do. Don't be impatient: remember, you can't warm your hands by burning your fingers.

Your success has less to do with speed, but more to do with timing and direction. The key is doing the right thing at the right time. Tryon Edwards said, "Have a time and place for everything, and do everything in its time and place, and you will not only accomplish more, but have far more leisure than those who are always hurrying." The problem is that many a "go-getter" never stops long enough to let opportunity catch up with them.

Lord Chesterfield said, "Whoever is in a hurry shows that the thing he is about is too big for him." When you are outside of the right timing, you will sow hurry and reap frustration. There is simply more to life than increasing its speed.

Brendon Francis commented, "Failure at a task may be the result of having tackled it at the wrong time." If the time has passed, preparation does no good. The trouble with life in the fast lane is that you get to the other end too soon. Soren Kierkegaard said, "Most men pursue pleasure with such breathless haste that they hurry past it." Haste makes waste; give time, time. Many people overestimate what they can do in a year and underestimate what they can do in a lifetime.

Bruyere said, "There is no road too long to the man who advances deliberately and without undo haste; no honor is too distant to the man who prepares himself for them with patience." Many times the action that you take at the right time has no immediate relationship to the answer—it's to get you to the right place at the right time.

We are happiest when we discover that what we should be doing and what we are doing are the same things. I agree with what the book of Ecclesiastes says: "To everything there is a season, a time for every purpose under heaven." You will never be what you ought to be until you are doing what you ought to be doing.

If you are facing the right direction, just keep on walking. Francis Bacon says, "The lame man who keeps the right road outstrips the runner who takes a wrong one . . . the more active and swift the latter is the further he will go astray." Determine to choose the right pace: if you go too fast, you can catch up with misfortune, and if you go too slow, misfortune can catch up with you. Be patient and persistent, then you will miss all the wrong places and end up where you're supposed to be.

ALWAYS SPEAK LESS THAN YOU KNOW.

Recently I saw a sign under a mounted large mouth bass. It read: "If I had kept my mouth shut I wouldn't be here." How true! Don't jump into trouble mouth first. What we say is important. The book of Job reminds us, "How forcible are right words." Let me pose this question for you: What would happen if you changed what you said about your biggest problem, your biggest opportunity?

Our daily commitment ought to be, "Oh please fill my mouth with worthwhile stuff, and nudge me when I've said enough." The human tongue is only a few inches from the brain, but when you listen to some people talk, they seem miles apart. The tongue runs fastest when the brain is in neutral.

A high school track coach was having difficulty motivating his team to perform at its best. The team developed the distinct reputation of coming in last at every track meet they entered. One factor contributing to his less than successful program was the coach's "pep talk" tactics. His most effective inspiring tool, he thought, was to tell his team, "Keep turning left and hurry back." Your words have the power to start fires or quench passion.

Choose to speak positive, motivating, pleasant words. Pascal commented, "Kind words do not cost much. They never blister the tongue or lips. Mental trouble was never known to arise from such quarters. Though they do not cost much, yet they accomplish much. They bring out a good nature in others. They also produce their own image on a man's soul, and what a beautiful image it is." Sir Wilfred Grenfell said, "Start some kind word on its travels. There is no telling where the good it may do will stop."

"The words 'I am' are potent words; be careful what you hitch them to. What you're claiming has a way of reaching back and claiming you" (A.L. Kietselman). Sometimes your biggest enemies and most trustworthy friends are the words you say to yourself. Proverbs is true: "Life and death are in the power of the tongue."

Henry Ward Beecher reflected, "A helping word to one in trouble is often like the switch on a railroad track . . . an inch between a wreck and smooth rolling prosperity." Johann Lavater said, "Never tell evil of a man if you do not know it for certain and if you know it for certain, then ask yourself, 'Why should I tell it?'"

What words have the most powerful effect on you? George Burnham said, " 'I can't do it' never accomplished anything. 'I will try' has performed wonders."

If your lips would keep from slips;

Five things observe with care;

To whom you speak, of whom you speak,

And how, and when, and where.

Nugget #36

In Trying Times, Don't Quit Trying.

"The world will always give you the opportunity to quit, but only the world would call quitting an opportunity" (Clint Brown). One of the most powerful success principles ever preached is: *Never give up!*

As an author, I have the privilege of signing many books. I like to write encouraging expressions in each book before I sign my name. One of my most common sayings is: *Never give up!* Joel Budd remarked, "It isn't the final say so, unless *you* say so." Richard Nixon mused, "A man is not finished when he is defeated. He is finished when he quits."

Nobody and nothing can keep you down unless you decide not to rise again. H.E. Jansen said, "The man who wins may have been counted out several times, but he didn't hear the referee." Find a way to, not a way *not* to.

A lazy man is always judged by what he doesn't do. The choice of giving up or going on is a defining moment in your life. You cannot turn back the clock. But you can wind it up again.

A couple of years ago, I had the privilege of meeting Peter Lowe, the founder of the very successful, *Success* seminars. As we talked, he commented, "The most common trait I have found in all people that are successful is that they have conquered the temptation to give up." One of the best ways to give your best a chance, is to rise up when you're knocked down.

Too many people stop faster than they start. Instead of stopping, follow this English proverb: "Don't fall before you are pushed." Margaret Thatcher understood the principle of not quitting when she advised, "You may have to fight a battle more than once to win it." David Zucker added, "Quit now, you'll never make it. If you disregard this advice you'll be halfway there."

"I can't!" is the conclusion of fools. Listen to Clare Booth Luce: "There are no hopeless situations, there are only men who have grown hopeless about them." Admiral Chester Nimitz remarked, "God grant me the courage not to give up what I think is right even though I think it is hopeless." Giving up is the ultimate tragedy. The famous boxer, Archie Moore, reflected, "If I don't get off the mat, I'll lose the fight."

The choice is simple. You can either stand up and be counted, or lie down and be counted out. Defeat never comes to people until they admit it. Your success will be measured by your willingness to keep on trying. Have the courage to live. Anyone can quit.

Nugget #37

ONLY HUNGRY MINDS CAN GROW.

Have you ever noticed how many people you know who are literally at the same place today as they were five years ago? They still have the same dreams, the same problems, the same alibis, the same opportunities. They are standing still in life.

It's as if people unplug their clocks at a certain point in time and stay at that fixed moment the rest of their lives. You are destined to grow, learn and improve. The biggest room in our lives is always the room for self-improvement.

A famous saying reads: "It's what you learn after you know it all that counts." I must admit that I am somewhat of a fanatic about this. I hate to have idle time–time in which I am not learning anything. Those around me know that I must always have something to read or write during any idle moment that might arise.

I try to learn from everyone. From one I may learn what not to do, while from another, I learn what to do. Learn from the mistakes of others. You can never live long enough to make all the mistakes yourself. You can learn more from a wise man when he is wrong than a fool who is right.

Goethe said, "Everybody wants to be: nobody wants to grow." I agree with Van Crouch: "You will never change your actions until you change your mind." An important way to keep growing is to never stop asking questions. Life's most important answers can be found in asking the right questions.

The person who is afraid of asking is ashamed of learning. Only hungry minds can grow. It's true what W. Fussellman said, "Today a reader. Tomorrow a leader."

We should learn as if we will live forever and live as if we are going to die tomorrow. Harvey Ullman said, "Anyone who stops learning is old, whether this happens at 20 or 80. Anyone who keeps on learning not only remains young, but becomes consistently more valuable regardless of physical capacity." It's fun to keep learning. Learning brings life to your life.

Learn from others. Learn to see in the challenges of others, the ills you should avoid. Experience is a present possession that keeps us from repeating the past in the future. Life teaches us by giving us new problems. Think education is expensive or difficult? Listen to Derek Bok: "If you think education is expensive–try ignorance."

BE YOURSELF. WHO ELSE IS BETTER QUALIFIED?

I have the opportunity to spend large segments of time in airports because I travel frequently. Almost invariably when in an airport, I notice scores of people who look like they are in a hurry to nowhere. Isn't it incredible that so many people devote their whole lives to fields of endeavor that have nothing to do with the gifts and talents inside them? Incredibly, many actually spend their entire lives trying to change the way they were made.

Every person has specific gifts, talents and strengths. The book of Corinthians asserts, "Each man has his own gift from God." Marcus Aurelieus said, "Take full account of the excellencies which you possess and in gratitude remember how you would hanker after them if you had them not."

Robert Quillen reflected, "If you count all your assets you'll always show a profit." Seize the opportunities to use your gifts. "Put yourself on view. This always brings your talents to light" (Baltasar Gracian). Never judge yourself by your weaknesses. I agree with Malcolm Forbes who claimed, "Too many people overvalue what they are not and undervalue what they are." You are richer than you think you are.

Nathaniel Emmons said, "One principle reason why men are so often useless is that they neglect their own profession or calling and divide and shift their attention among a multitude of objects and pursuits." Your best will always arise when you tap into the best gifts inside you. I agree with William Matthews when he said, "One well cultivated talent, deepened and enlarged, is worth 100 shallow faculties."

Too many people take only their wants into consideration, never their talents and abilities. Deep down inside, if you are a musician, then make music. If you are a teacher, teach. Be what you are and you will be at peace with yourself. I agree with William Boetecher who declared, "The more you learn what to do with yourself, and the more you do for others, the more you will learn to enjoy the abundant life." Do what's most natural for you. Deep inside we're all like what Yoruba said, "You can't stop a pig from wallowing in the mud."

E.E. Cummings advised, "To be nobody but yourself–in a world which is doing its best, night and day, to make you everybody else–means to fight the hardest battle which any human being can fight and never stop fighting." The bottom line is–be yourself!

I agree with Sydney Harris: "Ninety percent of the world's woe comes from people not knowing themselves, their abilities, their frailties and even their real virtues." Don't expect anything original from an echo. Musset said, "How glorious it is and also how painful–to be an exception." Billy Walder adds, "Trust your own instinct. Your mistakes might as well be your own, instead of someone else's." Abraham Lincoln said it best: "Whatever you are, be a good one."

Nugget #39

GO FROM . . .

Go from burnout to recharged.

Go from failure to learning.

Go from regrets of the past to dreams of the future.

Go from prejudice to reconciliation.

Go from ordinary to extraordinary.

Go from defective to effective.

Go from despiteful to insightful.

Go from whining to winning.

Go from lukewarm to "on fire".

Go from security to opportunity.

Go from fear to action.

Go from resisting to receiving.

Go from thinking of yourself to thinking of others.

Go from complaining to obtaining.

Go from drifting to steering.

Go from being a problem to being an answer.

Go from trying to committing.

Go from a copy to an original.

Go from envying others to serving others.

Go from ingratitude to thanksgiving.

Go from fault-finding to forgiveness.

Go from criticism to compliments.

Go from alibis to action.

Go from procrastination to progress.

Go from hesitation to obedience.

Go from blending in to standing out.

Go from fractured to focused.

Go from taking to giving.

Go from wishing to wisdom.

Nugget #40

GET UP ONE MORE TIME THAN YOU'VE FALLEN DOWN.

Have you ever failed or made a mistake? Good, then this nugget is for you. The fact that you've failed is proof that you're not finished. Failures and mistakes can be a bridge, not a barricade, to success. Successful people believe that mistakes are just feedback. It's not how far you fall but how high you bounce that makes all the difference.

Theodore Roosevelt said, "Far better it is to dare mighty things, to win glorious triumphs, even though checkered by failure than to rank with those poor spirits who neither enjoy much nor suffer much because they live in the great twilight that knows not victory or defeat." One of the riskiest things you can do in life is to take too many precautions and never have any failures or mistakes. Failure is the opportunity to start over more intelligently.

No one has ever achieved genuine success who did not, at one time or another, teeter on the edge of disaster. If you have tried to do something and failed, you are vastly better off than if you had tried to do nothing and succeeded. The person who never makes a mistake must get awfully tired of doing nothing. If you're not making mistakes, you're not risking enough.

Vernon Sanders says, "Experience is a hard teacher because she gives the test first, the lesson afterwards." Experience is what you get when you are looking for something else.

Success consists of getting up just one time more than you fall down. So get up and go on. Proverbs says, "A man who refuses to admit his mistakes can never be successful, but if he confesses and forsakes them, he gets another chance."

The death of your dream will not happen because of a failure. Its death will come from indifference and apathy. The best way to go on after a failure is to learn the lesson and forget the details. If you don't, you'll become like the scalded dog that fears hot water, and afterwards, cold.

Failure can become a weight or it can give you wings. The only way to make a comeback is to go on. If the truth were known, 99 percent of success is built on former failure. A mistake usually proves somebody stopped talking long enough to do something. You're like a tea bag: not worth much until you've been through some hot water.

Remember the old poem that says:

Success is failure turned inside out,
the silver tint of the clouds of doubt.

And you never can tell how close you are;
it may be near when seems so far.

So stick to the fight when you're hardest hit;
it's when things seem worse that you must not
quit.

(Unknown)

Nugget #41

AN OVERNIGHT SUCCESS TAKES ABOUT TEN YEARS.

Never give up on what you really know you should do. Failure is waiting on the path of least persistence. The "man of the hour" spent many days and nights getting there.

Consider the man who said, "My overnight success was the longest night of my life." Winners simply do what losers don't want to do longer.

Earl Nightingale said, "A young man once asked a great and famous older man, 'How can I make a name for myself in the world and become successful?' The great and famous man replied: 'You have only to decide upon what it is you want and then stay with it, never deviating from your course no matter how long it takes, or how rough the road, until you have accomplished it.'" Success is found by holding on long after others have let go.

The famous old saying is true: "In the confrontation between the stream and the rock, the stream always wins–not through strength but through perseverance." Christopher Morley said, "Big shots are only little shots that keep shooting." Persistence is simply enjoying the distance between the birth and fulfillment of your dreams.

We should be people of strong *wills*, not strong *won'ts*. Many of the world's great failures did not realize how close they were to success when they gave up. Stopping at third base adds no more score than striking out.

When you're persistent, it's proof you have not been defeated. Mike Murdock says, "You have no right to anything you have not pursued. For the proof of desire is in the pursuit." Life holds no greater wealth than that of steadfast commitment. It cannot be robbed from you. Only you can lose it by your will.

When faithfulness is most difficult, it is most necessary, because trying times are no time to quit trying. The secret of success is to start from scratch and keep on scratching. We rate success by what people finish, not by what they start. People do not fail, they just quit too easily.

A MAN WITHOUT PRINCIPLE NEVER DRAWS MUCH INTEREST.

D
o you know what this page is noted for? From this page you can go anywhere you want to. This page can be the springboard to your future. You can start here and begin to move forward.

"Eli Whitney was laughed at when he showed his cotton gin. Edison had to install his electric light free of charge in an office building before anyone would even look at it. The first sewing machine was smashed to pieces by a Boston mob. People scoffed at the idea of railroads. People thought that traveling thirty miles an hour would stop the circulation of the blood. Morse had to plead before ten Congresses before they would even look at his telegraph" (Anonymous). Yet for all these men the sky was not the limit. "Beware of those who stand aloof and greet each venture with reproof; the world would stop if things were run by men who say 'It can't be done.'" (Samuel Glover).

We achieve in proportion to what we attempt. More people are persuaded into believing in nothing than into believing too much. You are never as far from the answer as it first appears. It's never safe or accurate to look into the future without faith.

Each of us has the potential and opportunity for success. It takes just as much effort to lead an unproductive life as it does an effective life. It always costs more not to do what's right than to do it. Still, millions lead aimless lives in prisons of their own making—simply because they haven't decided what to do with their lives.

"A lot of people confuse bad decision-making with destiny" (Kin Hubbard). "Where there is no vision the people perish," says the book of Proverbs. It's not the absence of things that make you unhappy, but the absence of vision.

You can predict a person's future by their awareness of their destiny. Life's heaviest burden is to have nothing to carry. The impact of any person is determined by the cause for which they live and the price they are willing to pay. What you set your heart on will determine how you spend your life.

Do not take lightly the dreams and hopes you have for your life. Cherish them, for they are like children birthed within you. "It is better to die for something than it is to live for nothing," says Dr. Bob Jones, Sr. A man without principle never draws much interest.

A lot of people no longer hope for the best; they just hope to avoid the worst. Too many have heard opportunity knocking at their door, but by the time they unhooked the chain, pushed back the bolt, turned two locks and shut off the burglar alarm–it was gone! Too many people spend their lives looking around, looking down, or looking behind. Instead, look up, take the lid off, the sky's not the limit!

Nugget #43

DON'T SIT BACK AND TAKE WHAT COMES, GO AFTER WHAT YOU WANT.

Get aggressive and go after opportunities. They usually don't find you, you must find them. The reason most people don't go very far in life is because they sidestep opportunity and shake hands with procrastination. Procrastination is the grave in which opportunity is buried. Don't be out in the backyard looking for four-leaf clovers when opportunity knocks at your front door.

For the tenacious there is always time and opportunity. Are you waiting on opportunities, or are opportunities waiting on you? I believe you should take the initiative and live your life on the offensive. William Menninger said, "The amount of satisfaction you get from life depends largely on your own ingenuity, self-sufficiency, and resourcefulness. People who wait around for life to supply their satisfaction usually find boredom instead."

Albert Hubert remarked, "Parties who want milk should not seat themselves on a stool in the middle of the field and hope that the cow will back up to them." The door of opportunity won't open unless you push. It is always a bumpy, uphill road that leads to heights of greatness. Being on the defensive has never produced ultimate victory. Do like Sara Teasdale said, "I make the most of all that comes and the least of all that goes."

Helen Keller said, "Never bend your head. Hold it high. Look the world straight in the eyes." If you want success you must seize your own opportunities as you go. I agree with Jonathan Winters: "I couldn't wait for success—so I went ahead without it." Lillian Hellman said, "It is best to act with confidence, no matter how little right you have to it."

George Adams said, "In this life we only get those things for which we hunt, for which we strive and for which we are willing to sacrifice." Don't just face opportunities and problems, attack them. Consider what B. C. Forbes said: "Mediocre men wait for opportunities to come to them. Strong, able, alert men go after opportunity."

"A wise man will make more opportunities than he finds," said Francis Bacon. It's more valuable to find a situation that redistributes opportunity than one that redistributes money. Have you ever noticed that great people are never lacking for opportunities? When successful people are interviewed, they always mention their big plans for the future. Observing them, most people would think, "If I were in their shoes, I'd kick back and do nothing." Success doesn't diminish their desire for dreaming.

There is far more opportunity than ability. Life is full of golden opportunities. Every person has a lot that they can do. Start with what you can do; don't stop because of what you can't do. Great opportunities will come as you make the most of small ones. Many people seem to think that opportunity means a chance to get money without earning it. The best gifts we get are opportunities, not things. Seize them!

Nugget #44

HAVE . . .

Have peace enough to press on.

Have hope enough to keep your heart looking forward.

Have strength enough to battle obstacles and overcome them.

Have commitment enough to not give up too soon.

Have fun enough to enjoy every aspect of life.

Have patience enough to let faith complete its work in you.

Have love enough to give to those who deserve it the least but need it the most.

Have focus enough to say "no" to many good ideas.

Have forgiveness enough to never end the day hating someone.

Have honesty enough to never have to remember what you said.

Have character enough to do in the light what you would do in the dark.

Have gratitude enough to say "thank you" for the small things.

Have purpose enough to know *why* not just *how*.

Have perseverance enough to run the entire race that is set out before you.

Have responsibility enough to be the most dependable person you know.

Have kindness enough to share what you have and who you are with others.

Have mercy enough to forgive and forget.

Have devotion enough to do the right things on a daily basis.

Have courage enough to face and fight any opposition to what you know is right.

Have expectancy enough to be on the lookout for opportunities every day.

Have obedience enough to do what is right without thinking twice.

Have direction enough to know when and where to go.

Have knowledge enough to have your mind continually educated.

Have credibility enough to cause others to want to work together with you.

Have generosity enough to give before being asked.

Have compassion enough to be moved by the needs of others.

Have loyalty enough to be committed to others.

Nugget #45

DREAM ABOUT THE FUTURE AND ACT BEFORE IT OCCURS.

The person with imagination is never alone and never finished. You were created for creativity. Your eyes are designed to look for opportunity, your ears listen for direction, your mind requires a challenge and your heart longs for the best way.

Make a daily demand on your creativity. Everything great started as somebody's daydream. Successful people are first dreamers. The wonder of your imagination is this: it has the power to light its own fire. Ability is a flame, but creativity is a fire.

Originality sees things with fresh vision. Unlike an airplane, your imagination can take off day or night in any kind of circumstances. Let it fly!

A person of vision is someone who shoots at a target no one else sees and hits it. "We are told never to cross a bridge till we come to it, but this world is owned by men who have 'crossed bridges' in their imagination far ahead of the crowd" (Speakers Library).

Many times we act, or fail to act, not because of will but because of imagination. A person's dreams are an indicator of their potential greatness.

Grandmother saw Billy running around the house slapping himself and asked him why. "Well," said Billy, "I just got so tired of walking that I thought I'd ride my horse for a while." One day Michelangelo saw a block of marble that the owner said was of no value. "It is valuable to me," said Michelangelo. "There is an angel imprisoned in it, and I must set it free."

Other people may be smarter, better educated or more experienced than you, but no single person has an exclusive on dreams, desire or ambition. The creation of a thousand trees of opportunity spring from a tiny acorn of an idea.

"No man that does not see visions will ever realize any high hope or undertake any high enterprise," said Woodrow Wilson. Not being a person of imagination causes your life to be less than it was intended to be.

A dream is one of the most exciting things there is. Your heart has eyes that the brain knows nothing of. You are more than an empty bottle to be filled. You are a candle to be lit. Light the fire of your imagination. Dare to dream. Get caught creating.

Nugget #46

THERE'S NO BETTER EXCERCISE FOR THE HEART THAN HELPING SOMEONE UP.

What we do for ourselves alone dies with us; what we do for others is timeless. No one is more deceived or cheated than a selfish person. "No man was ever honored for what he received. Honor has been the reward for what he gave," said Calvin Coolidge. Invest in the success of others. When you help someone up a mountain, you'll find yourself close to the summit, too.

Proverbs says, "It is possible to give away and become richer! It is also possible to hold on too tightly and lose everything. Yes, the liberal man shall be rich! By watering others, he waters himself." "What I gave, I have; what I spent, I had; what I kept, I lost" (Old epitaph). You and I were created to help others.

If you treat a person as they are, they will remain the same. If you treat them as if they were what they could be, they can become what they could be. Practicing the Golden Rule is not a sacrifice; it's an incredible investment.

You grow to the extent that you give out. By giving out, you create more room to grow on the inside. So, don't give 'til it hurts; give 'til it feels good. Make this commitment: to leave others better than you found them.

If you want others to improve, let them hear the nice things you say about them. People will treat you the way you view them. Find the good in everyone. Draw out their talents and abilities. To lead people, let them know that you are behind them. It is the duty of all leaders to make it difficult for others to do wrong and easy to do right.

What means most in life is what you have done for others. Most people can smile for two months on five words of praise and a pat on the back. The best way to encourage yourself is to encourage someone else. "Those who bring sunshine to the lives of others cannot keep it from themselves," said James Matthew Barrie.

YOU CAN'T GET AHEAD WHEN YOU'RE TRYING TO GET EVEN.

Never cut what can be untied" (Joseph Joubert). When you have been wronged, a poor memory is your best response. Never carry a grudge. While you're straining under its weight, the person you're mad at is out producing.

Forgive your enemies—nothing annoys them more. There is no revenge so sweet as forgiveness. The only people you should try to get even with are those who have helped you.

"Forgiveness ought to be like a canceled note—torn in two, and burned up, so that it never can be shown against one" (Henry Ward Beecher). One of the greatest strengths you can show is when you forego revenge and dare to forgive an injury.

"He who cannot forgive, destroys the bridge over which he may one day need to pass," said Larry Bielat. The one guaranteed formula for limiting your potential is unforgiveness. Hate, bitterness and revenge are luxuries you cannot afford.

People need loving most when they deserve it least. Forgiveness heals; unforgiveness wounds. When we think about our offense, trouble grows; when we forgive, trouble goes.

When you don't forgive, you are ignoring its impact on your destiny. "Hate is a prolonged form of suicide" (Douglas V. Steere). How much more grievous are the consequences of unforgiveness than the causes of it! Norman Cousins summed it up when he said, "Life is an adventure in forgiveness."

It's true that the one who forgives ends the quarrel. Patting a fellow on the back is the best way to get a chip off his shoulder. Forgive your enemies—you can't get back at them any other way! Forgiveness saves the expense of anger, the high cost of hatred and the waste of energy. There are two marks of greatness: giving and forgiving.

If you want to be miserable, hate somebody. Unforgiveness does a great deal more damage to the vessel in which it is stored than the object on which it is poured. "Every person should have a special cemetery lot in which to bury the faults of friends and loved ones. To forgive is to set a prisoner free and discover the prisoner was you" (Unknown).

THE ROAD TO SUCCESS IS ALWAYS UNDER CONSTRUCTION.

The late astronaut James Irwin said, "You might think going to the moon was the most scientific project ever but they literally 'threw us' in the direction of the moon. We had to adjust our course every ten minutes and landed only inside fifty feet of the 500 mile radius of our target." On that mission, every change no matter how small, was essential to success.

"When you can't change the direction of the wind–adjust your sails" (Max DePree). We cannot become what we need to be by remaining what we are. People hate change, yet it is the only thing that brings growth. There is nothing so permanent as change.

Everyone wants to change the world, but no one thinks of changing himself. "Poverty and shame shall be to him that refuses instruction: but he that regards reproof shall be honored" (Proverbs).

Unacceptance of your present creates a future. "Better to be pruned to grow than cut up to burn," said John Trapp. A bad habit never goes away by itself. "It's always an undo-it-yourself project" (Abigail Van Buren).

Wise people sometimes change their minds–fools never do. Be open to changes in your plans. It is a sign of strength to make changes when necessary.

The longer a person is in error, the surer they are they are right and the less open they are to change. Defending your faults and errors only proves that you have no intention of quitting them. An obstinate man does not hold opinions–they hold him.

Where we cannot invent we can at least improve. A "sensational new idea" is sometimes just an old idea with its sleeves rolled up. If you itch for ideas, keep on scratching. Don't be afraid of change.

Everybody is in favor of progress; it's the change they don't like. Face it, constant change is here to stay. Most people are willing to change, not because they see the light, but because they feel the heat.

Great ideas still need change, adaptation and modification in order to prosper and succeed. Henry Ford forgot to put a reverse gear in his first automobile (it would get you there, but you couldn't get back). Few knew of his oversight. Because he changed, few don't know of his success. Success and growth are unlikely if you always do things the way you've always done them. When you stop changing, you stop growing.

THE PERSON WHO FINDS THE NEGATIVE SELDOM FINDS ANYTHING ELSE.

Just to see how it feels, for the next twenty-four hours refrain from saying anything bad about anyone or anything. "The difference between the right word and almost the right word is the difference between lightning and the lightning bug," said Mark Twain.

Your words reflect what you believe about your future. A leader says, "Let's find a way;" a loser says, "There is no way." A leader says, "There should be a better way to do it;" a loser says, "That's the way it's always been done." Instead of using the words "if only", try substituting "next time". Don't ask, "What if it doesn't work?" Ask instead, "What if it does?"

Ignorance is always eager to speak. The best time to hold your tongue is when you feel you must say something. You're unlikely to be hurt by anything you didn't say. Never judge a person's horsepower by their exhaust. Some people speak from experience; others, from experience, don't speak.

We all should take a tip from nature–our ears aren't made to shut, but our mouth is! When an argument flares up, the wise person quenches it with silence. Silence is the ultimate weapon of power; it is also one of the hardest arguments to dispute. Sometimes you have to be quiet to be heard.

The person who finds the negative seldom finds anything else. Live your life as an exclamation, not an explanation. Children are born optimists, then the world slowly tries to educate them out of their "delusion." The fact is, the more you complain the less you'll obtain. A life of complaining is the ultimate rut. The only difference between a rut and a grave is the timing.

Some people always find the bad in a situation. Do you know people like that? How many successful complainers do you know? "Little men with little minds and little imagination go through life in little ruts, smugly resisting all changes which would jar their little worlds" (Anonymous). Small things affect small minds.

Has your dream become your hope or your excuse? Don't complain. The wheel that squeaks the loudest often gets replaced. Flapping gums dull your two most important senses—your sight and sound. Many a great idea has been quenched by wrong words. Don't spend your life standing at the complaint counter.

A wise old owl sat on an oak,

The more he saw the less he spoke;

The less he spoke the more he heard;

Why aren't we like that wise old bird?

(Edward H. Richards)

Nugget #50

WHAT WE TAKE FOR GRANTED TODAY SEEMED IMPOSSIBLE YESTERDAY.

Be bold and courageous. When you look back on your life, you'll regret the things you didn't do more than the ones you did. When facing a difficult task, act as though it is impossible to fail. If you're going to climb Mount Everest, bring along the American flag. Go out on a limb–that's where the fruit is.

Go from looking at what you can see to believing what you can have. Here's some life-changing advice: don't undertake a plan unless it is distinctly important and nearly impossible. Don't bunt–aim out of the ballpark.

The mediocre man thinks he isn't. But, "Not doing more than the average is what keeps the average down," says William M. Winans. "Undertake something that is difficult; it will do you good. Unless you try to do something beyond what you have already mastered, you will never grow," said Ronald E. Osborn.

It is difficult to say what is truly impossible, for what we take for granted today seemed impossible yesterday. "Impossible," Napoleon is quoted as saying, "is a word found only in the dictionary of fools." What words are found in your dictionary?

He who is afraid of doing too much always does too little. To achieve all that is possible, we must attempt the impossible. Your vision must be bigger than you. Learn to be comfortable with great dreams.

The best jobs haven't been found. The best work hasn't been done. Unless you take on more than you can possibly do, you will never do all that you can. Don't listen to those who say, "It's not done that way." Don't listen to those who say, "You're taking too big a chance." Develop an infinite capacity to ignore what others say can't be done.

If Michelangelo had painted the floor instead of the ceiling of the Sistine Chapel, it would surely be rubbed out by today. "Always aim high, going after things that will make a difference rather than seeking the safe path of mediocrity," says Wess Roberts.

Don't bother with small plans, because they motivate no one (especially you!). The person who expects nothing will never be disappointed. After Roger Bannister broke the four-minute mile, within one year thirty-seven others broke it; within two years three hundred had broken it. Thinking high affects others.

The most disappointed people in the world are those who get just what is coming to them and no more. There are a lot of ways to become a failure, but never taking a chance is the most successful.

Nugget #51

START WITH WHAT YOU HAVE; DON'T WAIT ON WHAT YOU DON'T HAVE.

You already have been given what you need to begin to create your future. Don't find yourself saying, "If only I had this . . . if only this were different . . . if only I had more money, then I could do what I am supposed to do." People always overstate the importance of things they don't have.

Never let what you think you can't do keep you from doing what you can do. Prolonged idleness paralyzes initiative, because to the hesitant mind, everything is impossible because it seems so.

Do not wait for special circumstances to act; use ordinary situations. We don't need more strength, ability or greater opportunity. Use what you have. Everyone must row with the oars they have been given.

"The lure of the distant and the difficult is deceptive. The great opportunity is where you are," said John Burroughs. What you can do now is the only influence you have over your future. No one can be happy until they have learned to enjoy what they have and not worry over what they don't have.

True greatness consists of being great in little things. Don't grumble because you don't have what you want; be thankful you don't get what you deserve. "'We must do something' is the unanimous refrain. 'You begin' is the deafening reply," said Walter Dwight.

It is right to be content with what you have, never with what you are. Happiness will never come to those who fail to appreciate what they already have. Don't make the mistake of looking too far ahead and miss the things close by.

You can never get much of anything done unless you go ahead and do it before everything is perfect. No one ever made a success of anything by first waiting until all the conditions were "just right."

It's a waste of time to think about what you don't have. Instead, spend your time in the task before you, knowing that the right performance of this hour's duties will be the best preparation for the years that follow it. Live this German proverb: "Grow where you are planted. Begin to weave, and God will give the thread."

Nugget #52

THERE IS NO RIGHT WAY TO DO A WRONG THING.

Commit yourself to excellence from the start. No legacy is so rich as excellence. The quality of your life will be in direct proportion to your commitment to excellence, regardless of what you choose to do. "It's a funny thing about life; if you refuse to accept anything but the best, you very often get it," said Somerset Maugham.

It takes less time to do something right than it does to explain why you did it wrong. There is no right way to do the wrong thing. "There is an infinite difference between a little wrong and just right, between fairly good and the best, between mediocrity and superiority," said Orison Marden.

Every day we should ask ourselves, "Why should I be hired instead of someone else?" or "Why should people do business with me instead of my competitors?" "Watch your actions; they become habits. Watch your habits; they become character. Watch your character; it becomes your destiny," said Frank Outlaw.

To be excellent, be honest. Those who are given to white lies soon become color blind. When you stretch the truth, watch out for the snap back. A lie has no legs to support itself–it requires other lies. Beware of a half-truth; you may get a hold of the wrong half.

Each time you are honest, you propel yourself toward greater success. Each time you lie, even a little white lie, you push yourself toward failure.

Outside forces don't control your character, you do. The measure of a person's real character is what he would do if he knew he would never be found out.

In the race for excellence, there is no finish line. Be more concerned with your character than with your reputation. Your character is what you really are while your reputation is merely what others think you are.

"He that is good will infallibly become better, and he that is bad will as certainly become worse; for vice, virtue and time are three things that never stand still," said Charles Caleb Colton. Recently I saw a plaque that said, "Excellence can be attained if you . . . Care more than others think is wise, Risk more than others think is safe, Dream more than others think is practical, Expect more than others think is possible." Excellence—it's contagious. Start an epidemic!

Nugget #53

THE MORE YOU LOOK BACKWARD, THE LESS YOU'LL SEE FORWARD.

Yesterday ended last night. So, today it is more valuable to look ahead and prepare than to look back and regret. Don't let regrets replace your dreams. "A man is not old until regrets take the place of dreams" (John Barrymore). Regret looks back. Worry looks around. Vision looks up.

Life can be understood backward, but it must be lived forward. If past history were all that mattered, librarians would be the only successful people in the world. The past should only be viewed with gratitude for the good things. So, look backward with gratitude and forward with confidence. Your past is the start of your fresh start.

Consider what Vivian Laramore said, "I've shut the door on yesterday and thrown the key away–tomorrow holds no fears for me, since I've found today." Use the past as a launching pad, not a lawn chair. Dreams of the future are more valuable than the history of the past.

Experience is at best yesterday's answer to today's problem. Your past is not your potential. Never build your future around your past. The past is over. To succeed, you must be willing to shed part of your previous life.

"Keep your eye on the road, and use your rear-view mirror only to avoid trouble" (Daniel Meacham). Stop taking journeys into the past. Don't make the mistake of letting yesterday use up too much of today.

It is more valuable to look where you're going than to see where you've been. Don't see your future only from the perspective of yesterday. It's too easy to limit everything and hinder the dream within you. "The past should be a springboard, not a hammock," said Edmund Burke. You can never plan the future by just looking at the past. Those to whom yesterday still looks big aren't doing much today.

Your future contains more happiness than any past you can remember. Don't look at your past to determine your future. You can't walk backward into the future. True misery can be found by being a yesterday person trying to get along with a tomorrow world. Don't let your past mistakes become memorials. They should be cremated, not embalmed.

Those who predominantly talk about the past are going backward. Those who talk about the present are usually just maintaining. But those who talk about the future are growing.

Some people stay so far in the past that the future is gone before they get there. The future frightens only those who prefer living in the past. No one has ever backed into prosperity. You can't have a better tomorrow if you are thinking about yesterday today. Yesterday has passed forever and is beyond our control. What lies behind us is insignificant compared to what lies ahead.

URGENT SELDOM IS.

"Time sure changes things," an airline passenger told his companion. "When I was a boy I used to sit in a flat bottom rowboat and fish in the lake down there below us. Every time a plane flew over, I'd look up and wish I were in it. Now I look down and wish I were fishing."

Being at the right place at the right time makes all the difference. How important is timing? Theodore Roosevelt said, "Nine-tenths of wisdom is being wise in time."

The fact that you're reading this book shows that you want to grow–to get somewhere. Like most of us, you want to get there as fast as you can. But, keep in mind that too swift is as untimely as too slow.

The situation that seems urgent seldom is. Haste slows every dream and opens the door to failure. "The more haste, the less speed" (John Heywood).

It's more important to know where you're going, than to see how fast you can get there. "Impatient people always get there too late" (Jean Dutourd). We undo ourselves by impatience.

One of the most frequent causes for the failure is impatience in waiting for results. "The haste of a fool is the slowest thing in the world" (Thomas Shadwell). If you find yourself in a hurry, it usually shows that the thing you're doing is too big for you.

"There is a time to let things happen and a time to make things happen" (Hugh Prather). Life is lived in seasons, which means that we can succeed best by doing different things at different times.

Do the right thing at the right time. A Chinese proverb says, "Never leave your field in spring or your house in winter." There is never a winter that's not followed with the joy of spring, the growth of summer and the harvest of fall.

Finish strong; no one remembers the score at half-time. Never claim a victory prematurely. The greatest assassin of dreams is haste, the desire to reach things before the right time. There's a lot you can learn while you wait. Impatience is one big "get-ahead-ache."

Nugget #55

TO FINISH THE RACE, STAY ON THE TRACK.

O pportunity is all around you. What matters is where you put your focus. Ask yourself this question every day: "Where should my focus be?" Where you focus your attention, you create strength and momentum.

These are the characteristics of momentum: (1) it is single-minded; (2) it is unwavering in the pursuit of a goal; (3) it has passion which knows no limits; (4) it demands a concentrated intensity and a definite sense of destiny; and most of all, (5) it has a boundless vision and commitment to excellence.

Concentration is the key that opens the door to accomplishment. "The first law of success . . . is concentration–to bend all the energies to one point, and to go directly to that point, looking neither to the right nor to the left" (William Mathews).

The most successful people have always been those of concentration, who have struck their blows in one place until they have accomplished their purpose. They are of one specific idea, one steady aim, a single and concentrated purpose. Become an authority on something.

There is a great distance between most people's dreams and the results they achieve. It is due to the difference in their commitment to bring together all the options of their ability and to focus them upon one point.

There are two quick ways to disaster: taking nobody's advice and taking everybody's advice. Learn to say no to the good so you can say yes to the best. A.P. Goethe said that, in order to succeed, you must know three things: "(1) what to eliminate; (2) what to preserve; (3) when to say no, for developing the power to say no gives us the capacity to say yes."

We accomplish things by directing our desires, not by ignoring them. What an immense power you will have over your life when you possess distinct aims. Your words, the tone of your voice, your dress, your very motions change and improve when you begin to live for a reason.

Don't be a person who is uncertain about the future and hazy about the present. Stay in the groove without making it a rut. Make something your specialty. You cannot find until you define. To finish the race, stay on the track.

I am astonished at the aimlessness of most people's lives. As a result of a lack of focus, they delegate the direction of their lives to others. Don't live your life like that. Instead, "learn to define yourself, to content yourself with some specific thing and some definite work; dare to be what you really are, and to learn to accept with good grace all that you are not" (Anonymous).

STICKS AND STONES ARE ONLY THROWN AT FRUIT-BEARING TREES.

People with momentum all share one trait; they attract criticism. How you respond to that criticism will determine the rate of your momentum. I was reading a cover story on Billy Graham in *Time* magazine recently and was surprised to find in that article several criticisms of him from fellow ministers. I was reminded of this fact: all great people get great criticism. Learn to accept and expect the unjust criticisms for your great goals and accomplishments.

It can be beneficial to receive constructive criticism from those who have your best interests at heart, but you're not responsible to respond to those who don't. Don't ever give time to a critic; instead, invest it with a friend. I like what Edward Gibbon said: "I never make the mistake of arguing with people for whose opinions I have no respect."

It's a thousand times easier to criticize than create. That's why critics are never problem solvers. "Any fool can criticize, condemn and complain, and most do" (Dale Carnegie). My feeling is that the person who says it cannot be done, should not interrupt the one who is doing it. Just remember, when you are kicked from behind, it means you are out in front. A Yiddish proverb says, "A critic is like the girl who can't dance so she says the band can't play."

Critics know the answers without having probed deep enough to know the questions. "A critic is a man created to praise greater men than himself, but he is never able to find them" (Richard LeGallienne). The critic is convinced that the chief purpose of sunshine is to cast shadows. He doesn't believe anything, but he still wants you to believe him. Like a cynic, he always knows the "price of everything and the value of nothing" (Oscar Wilde). Don't waste time responding to your critics, because you owe nothing to a critic.

Don't belittle--be big; don't become a critic. "We have no more right to put our discordant states of mind into the lives of those around us and rob them of their sunshine and brightness than we have to enter their houses and steal their silverware" (Julia Seton). In criticizing others, remember that you will work overtime for no pay.

Never throw mud. If you do, you may hit your mark, but you will have dirty hands. Don't be a cloud because you failed to become a star. Instead, "Give so much time to the improvement of yourself that you have no time to criticize others" (Optimist Creed). Spend your time and energy creating, not criticizing.

A good thing to remember,

A better thing to do--

Work with the construction gang,

Not the wrecking crew.

(Anonymous)

Nugget #57

NOTHING IS MORE EXHAUSTING THAN SEARCHING FOR EASY WAYS TO EARN A LIVING.

"People judge you by your actions, not your intentions. You may have a heart of gold, but so does a hard boiled egg" (*Good Reading*). A thousand words will not leave as lasting an impression as one deed. Connect your good intentions with awesome actions. If you don't do it, you don't really believe it.

Some people spend their whole time searching for what's right, but then they can't seem to find any time to practice it. Remember, knowing what is right to do and then not doing it is wrong. Your life story is not written with a pen, but with your actions. To *do* nothing is the way to *be* nothing.

Action subdues fear. When we challenge our fears, we master them. When we wrestle with our problems, they lose their grip on us. When we dare to confront the things that scare us, we open the door to personal liberty.

Momentum doesn't just happen. "The common conception is that motivation leads to action, but the reverse is true–action precedes motivation" (Robert McKain). Don't wait to be motivated. "Take the bull by the horns until you have him screaming for mercy" (Michael Cadena).

Laziness is a load. Expectation is the idle man's income. Ironically, idleness is persistent. It keeps on and on, but soon enough it arrives at poverty.

"There is no idleness without a thousand troubles" (Welsh proverb). We are weakest when we try to get something for nothing. Proverbs says, "Hard work brings prosperity; playing around brings poverty."

Henry Ford once commented, "You can't build a reputation on what you're going to do." "Shun idleness. It is a rust that attaches itself to the most brilliant of metals" (Voltaire). We need to be like a cross between a carrier pigeon and a woodpecker: he not only carries the message, but he also knocks on the door.

A man of words and not of deeds is like a flower bed full of weeds. Don't let weeds grow around your dreams. To only dream of the person you would like to be is to waste the person you are. Don't just dream of great accomplishments; stay awake and do them.

Do more than exist, live.

Do more than hear, listen.

Do more than agree, cooperate.

Do more than talk, communicate.

Do more than grow, bloom.

Do more than spend, invest.

Do more than think, create.

Do more than work, excel.

Do more than share, give.

Do more than decide, discern.

Do more than consider, commit.

Do more than forgive, forget.

Do more than help, serve.

Do more than coexist, reconcile.

Do more than think, plan.

Do more than dream, do.

Do more than see, perceive.

Do more than read, apply.

Do more than receive, reciprocate.

Do more than choose, focus.

Do more than wish, believe.

Do more than advise, help.

Do more than speak, impart.

Do more than encourage, inspire.

Do more than add, multiply.

Do more than change, improve.

Do more than reach, stretch.

Nugget #59

GET CAUGHT DREAMING.

Stop and daydream once in awhile. Let your imagination roam and give it a chance to breathe. It's never too late for you to start thinking more creatively. Often it is just a lack of imagination that keeps a person from their potential. Thinking of new ideas is like shaving: if you don't do it every day, you're a bum. Have a constant flow of new, exciting and powerful ideas in your life.

Constantly frustrate tradition with your creativity and imagination. "The opportunities of man are limited only by his imagination. But so few have imagination that there are ten thousand fiddlers to one composer" (Charles Kettering). Your dreams are a preview to your greatness.

Those who do most, dream most. Dexter Yager says, "Don't let anybody steal your dream." A shallow thinker seldom makes a deep impression. We act, or fail to act, not because of *will*, as is so commonly believed, but because of *vision*. Only when you see the invisible can you do the impossible.

"Ideas are like rabbits. You get a couple and learn how to handle them, and pretty soon you have a dozen" (Anonymous). You'll get more out of every part of your life if you stay incurably curious. "The important thing is to not stop questioning. Never lose a holy curiosity" (Albert Einstein).

"We've got to have a dream if we are going to make a dream come true" (Denis Waitley). Nothing happens unless there's a dream first. The more you can dream, the more you can do. "Ideas are like the stars: we never reach them, but, like the mariners of the sea, we chart our course by them" (Carl Schurz). "Since it doesn't cost a dime to dream, you'll never short-change yourself when you stretch your imagination" (Robert Schuller). Look at things not as they are, but as they can be. Vision adds value to everything. A single idea—the sudden flash of any thought—may be worth a million dollars.

I believe we live in an unfinished world so we might share in the joys and satisfaction of creation. Creativity is built into every one of us; it's part of our design. Each of us lives less of the life intended for us when we choose not to use the creative powers we possess.

"I'm a big fan of dreams. Unfortunately, dreams are the first casualty in life—people seem to give them up quicker than anything for a 'reality'" (Kevin Costner). "Realistic people with practical aims are rarely as realistic or practical in the long-run of life as the dreamers who pursue their dreams" (Hans Selye). What you need is an idea. Be brave enough to live creatively.

WHAT YOU CAN DO–
YOU CAN *DO*.

W hat works? Work on that. Don't wish you could do things you can't do. Instead, think of what you can do.

Everyone who got where he is, had to begin where he was. Only one person in a thousand knows how to really live in the present. The problem is that we seldom think of what we have; instead, we think of what we lack.

"We don't need more strength or more ability or greater opportunity. What we need to use is what we have" (Basil Walsh). People are always ignoring something they can do and trying to do something they can't. Learning new things won't help the person who isn't using what he already knows. Success means doing the best we can with what we have.

Norman Vincent Peale said, "We've all heard that we have to learn from our mistakes, but I think it is more important to learn from our successes. If you learn only from your mistakes, you are inclined to learn only errors." In fact, some people spend their whole lives failing and never even notice.

The main thing that's wrong with doing nothing is that you never know when you are finished. When you are through improving, you're through. Use whatever you have been given, and more will come to you. Never leave well enough alone.

"Opportunities multiply as they are seized; they die when neglected" (Anonymous). "Every ceiling, when reached, becomes a floor upon which one walks and now can see a new ceiling. Every exit is an entry somewhere" (Tom Stoppard).

"You can't control the weather, but you can control the moral atmosphere that surrounds you. Why worry about things you can't control? Get busy controlling the things that depend upon you" (*In a Nutshell*). "A strong, successful man is not the victim of his environment. He creates favorable conditions" (Orsen Marden).

The best way to better your lot is to do a lot better. Build on the lot in life that you've been given. The person who gets ahead is the one who does more than is necessary—and keeps on doing it. No matter how rough the path, some press ahead; no matter how easy the going, some lag behind. Begin somewhere. You cannot fulfill your destiny on what you intend to do.

IF YOU HAVE A DESIRE,
DISTANCE DOESN'T MATTER.

The starting point of all accomplishment is desire. Keep this in mind: feeble desires bring feeble results just as a small amount of fire makes a small amount of heat. Be passionate about your life. Act from your passions. The more energy you apply to any task, the more you will have to apply to the next task.

Desire is like the planting of a seed. It causes something to begin and grow. Deep desire creates not only its own opportunities, but its own talents. Attitudes alter abilities.

It's passion that persuades. "A strong passion for any object will insure success, for the desire of the end will point out the means" (William Hazlitt).

The trouble with many educated men is that learning goes to their heads and not to their hearts. Does the path you're traveling capture your heart? You have been sent into this world to do something into which you can pour your heart.

You will only be remembered in life for your passions. Find something that consumes you. A belief is not just an idea a person possesses; it is an idea that possesses a person. Learn to be comfortable with being enthusiastic.

Every time zeal and passion are discussed someone brings up *balance*. Balance is a tremendous virtue, but the immediate neighbors of balance are apathy and weakness. If the truth were known, being balanced is usually an excuse for being lukewarm, indifferent or neutral. Indifference, lukewarmness, and neutrality are always attached to failure.

Enthusiasm can achieve in one day what it takes centuries to achieve by reason. "Above all else, guard your affections. For they influence everything else in your life" (Proverbs). William

James said, "Perhaps the greatest discovery of this century is that if you change your attitude, you can change your life."

Put a smile on what you do. It adds to your face value. When your enthusiasm increases, stress and fear in your life diminish. Passion is powerful.

"Believing is seeing. It's much more effective than the old notion that seeing is believing" (Terrence Deal). Love the thing you do, and you will keep doing better and bigger things.

Nugget #62

BE USED FOR A MIGHTY PURPOSE BIGGER THAN YOU.

People nearly always pick a problem their own size and ignore or leave to others the bigger or smaller ones. Pick a problem that's bigger than you. "Success, real success, in any endeavor demands more from an individual than most people are willing to offer–not more than they are capable of offering" (James Roche).

The desire for safety stands against every great and virtuous dream. Security, many times, is the first step towards stagnation. The trouble with this world is that too many people try to go through life with a catcher's mitt on both hands.

Boldness in vision is the first, second and third most important thing. If you dare nothing you should expect nothing.

"One who is contented with what he has done will never be famous for what he will do" (Christian Bovee). If you have achieved all you have planned for yourself, you have not planned enough.

Be used for something significant. Dare to do what's right for you. Choose a goal for which you are willing to exchange a piece of your life.

The surest way to happiness is to lose yourself in a cause greater than yourself. You'll be unhappy if you do not reach for something beyond yourself. If God is your partner, make your plans BIG.

"It is difficult to say what is impossible, for the dream of yesterday is the hope of today and the reality of tomorrow" (Robert Goddard). Every great action is impossible when it is undertaken. Only after it has become accomplished does it seem possible to the average man.

To small thinkers, everything looks like a mountain. The grandest things are, in some ways, the easiest to do because there is so little competition.

To be completely satisfied with yourself is a sure sign that progress is about to end. If you are satisfied with yourself, you'd better change your ideals. "How much better to know that we have dared to live our dreams than to live our lives in a lethargy of regret" (Gilbert Caplin).

You'll never succeed beyond your wildest dreams unless you have some wild dreams.

YOU WERE MADE ON PURPOSE FOR A PURPOSE.

The world makes room for a person of purpose. Their words and actions demonstrate that they know where they are going. You are built to conquer circumstances, solve problems and attain goals. You'll find no real satisfaction or happiness in life without obstacles to conquer, goals to achieve and a purpose to accomplish.

People say they want riches; what they need is fulfillment of a purpose. Happiness comes when we abandon ourselves for a purpose.

In your heart there is a sleeping lion called purpose. Every person alive has a destiny. Be on a mission. Have a definite sense of direction and purpose for your life. Successful lives are motivated by dynamic purpose. Strong convictions precede great actions.

As soon as you resign yourself to fate, your resignation is promptly accepted. You don't have a fate; you have a purpose. When you look into the future, you'll see it's so bright it'll make you squint. I'm encouraged by George Elliott, who said, "It's never too late to be what you might have been."

"More men fail through lack of purpose than lack of talent" (Billy Sunday). If your method is "hit or miss", you'll usually miss, because, "If you're not sure where you are going, you'll probably end up someplace else" (Robert F. Mager).

Don't be a person who doesn't know where you're going, but you're on your way. Growth for the sake of growth is the ideology of the cancer cell. Instead, go forward with definite purpose.

Lord Chesterfield wrote, "Firmness of purpose is one of the most necessary sinews of character and one of the best instruments of success. Without it, genius wastes its efforts in a maze of inconsistencies."

The person who has no direction is a slave of his circumstances. The poorest person is not someone without money, but without purpose. Without purpose, the only thing you can do is grow older.

"If you don't have a vision for your life, then you probably haven't focused in on anything" (Dr. David Burns). In the absence of vision there can be no clear and constant focus.

Once your purpose is clear, decisions will jump at you. "When you discover your mission, you will feel its demand. It will fill you with enthusiasm and a burning desire to get to work on it" (W. Clement Stone).

Nugget #64

ARE YOU READY?

To one person the world is desolate, dull and empty; to another the same world looks rich, interesting and full of meaning. "Eyes that look are common. Eyes that see are rare," says J. Oswald Sanders. How we position ourselves to see makes all the difference. You can never see the sunrise by looking to the west. The choice is up to you.

If you look at life the wrong way there is always cause for alarm. It's the same way a twenty dollar bill can look so big when it goes to church and so small when it goes for groceries. What you see depends mainly on what you look for. Some people complain because roses have thorns. Instead, be thankful that thorns have roses.

Position yourself to receive, not resist. How you see things on the outside of you depends on how things are on the inside of you. "Any fact facing us is not as important as our attitude toward it, for that determines our success or failure" (Norman Vincent Peale). Don't pray for rain, if you're going to complain about the mud.

"You and I do not see things as they are. We see things as we are" (Herb Cohen). Develop the hunter's approach; the outlook that wherever you go there are ideas waiting to be discovered. When you are positioned right, opportunity presents itself. Opportunities can drop in your lap if you have your lap where opportunities drop.

Opportunity can be missed if you are broadcasting when you should be tuning in. When opportunity knocks, some people object to the interruption. "One of the greatest and most comforting truths is that when one door opens, another closes, but often we look so long and regretfully upon the closed door that we do not see the one that is open for us" (Anonymous).

See success where others see only failure. Expect something good to happen. That expectation will energize your dreams and give them momentum.

You'll gain the advantage by doing things before they need to be done—positioning yourself ahead of time. You'll enjoy ongoing success when you travel a little bit in advance of the crowd.

I believe one of the major benefits of reading great books is that they can teach us how to respond in advance to many of life's challenges and opportunities. Great information can lead you to "dig a well before you are thirsty and plant a seed before you are hungry."

The trouble with the future for most people is it arrives before they are ready for it. Positioning yourself to receive causes you to be ready. Consider this important question: Are you ready?

You'll find that life responds to your outlook. We go where our vision is. Life is mostly a matter of expectation.

Nugget #65

GIVE BIRTH TO YOURSELF.

Do you want to stand out in the world? Then be yourself. Be what you really are. This is the first step toward becoming better than what you are now.

You and I are born equal but also different. "No man could be ideally successful until he has found his place. Like a locomotive, he is strong on the track, but weak anywhere else" (Orsen Marden). Choose to become yourself.

Avoid following the crowd. Be an engine, not a caboose. As Herman Melville wrote: "It is better to fail in originality than to succeed in imitation." Average people would rather be wrong than be different.

Conformity is the enemy of growth and satisfaction. Did you know you're destined to be different? Dare to be different and follow your own star.

"Be yourself. Who else is better qualified?" (Frank Giblin). Ask yourself these questions. If I try to be like him, who will be like me? If I'm not me, who will I be? The more you develop your potential, the less you will become like someone else. As long as you are trying to be like someone else, the best you can ever be is number two.

Trying to be like someone else is self-defeating. One of your main purposes in life is to give birth to yourself. Depend on what the book of Romans says, "God has given each of us an ability to do certain things well."

We can't reach our destiny taking another man's road. If you never walk except where you see another person's tracks, you will make no new discoveries for yourself. "Do not follow where the path may lead–go instead where there is no path and leave a trail" (Unknown).

You can't be common. The common go nowhere. You must be uncommon to be a champion. Your responsibility is not to remake yourself, but to make the absolute best of what you're made of.

Don't compromise yourself . . . it's all you've got. "Almost every man wastes part of his life in attempts to display qualities he does not possess" (Samuel Johnson). Don't let your life be a continual struggle to be what you are not, and to do what you should not.

"The more you are like yourself, the less you are like anyone else" (Walt Disney). You're like a tree–you must put forth the fruit that's created in you.

Nugget #66

IF YOU DON'T DECIDE WHAT'S IMPORTANT IN YOUR LIFE, SOMEONE ELSE WILL DECIDE FOR YOU.

Your destiny is not a matter of chance; it is a matter of choice. Many people have the right aims in life–they just never get around to pulling the trigger. You have to know what you want in order to attain it.

Harvey Cox said, "Not to decide is to decide." Weeds grow easily in the soil of indecision. Get out of the middle of the road. Standing in the middle of the road is very dangerous; you can get knocked down by traffic going both directions. The train of failure runs on the track of indecision.

Because of indecision, you can die before you're actually dead. "Indecision is debilitating; it feeds upon itself; it is, one might say, habit forming. Not only that, but it is contagious; it transmits itself to others" (H. A. Hopf).

A man with one watch knows what time it is; a man with two is never quite sure. Until you are decisively committed, there is hesitancy and the chance to draw back, followed by ineffectiveness. Listen to what you say. If you hear yourself saying, "I've decided," you're on the path towards an exciting and productive life.

Leaders have wills, not just wishes. The greater degree of wishful thinking, the greater degree of mediocrity. The weak are always forced to decide between alternatives that others have set before them, not the ones they've chosen for themselves. This lifestyle will leave you unhappy. However, consider what Mike Murdock says, "You have no right to complain about what you permit."

131

A wise person makes his own decisions; an ignorant one follows public opinion. Don't worry about not making a decision; someone else will make it for you. You are where you are today because of the choices you've made and haven't made. "The average man does not know what to do with this life, yet wants another one which will last forever," said Anatole France.

Results and success follow commitment and decisions. The result is that one decisive person always accomplishes more than a hundred people with just an interest. Decisions are what transforms an idea into a reality.

Be decisive even if it means you'll sometimes be wrong. A key to your future is that you can still choose, you can still decide. What you commit yourself to be will change you from what you are into what you can be. Decision determines destiny.

Nugget #67

EAGLES FLY ALONE; CROWS FLY IN GROUPS.

Every great idea and dream must be established within you and you alone. There will come times when only you will believe it is going to happen. Can you stand alone? Can you believe when it looks as if no one else does?

John Gardner declared, "The cynic says, 'One man can't do anything.' I say, 'Only one man can do anything.'" Nobody can do it for you. No one will do it for you.

Henry Wadsworth Longfellow puts it this way: "Not in the clamor of the crowded streets, not in the shouts or plaudits of the throng, but in ourselves are triumph and defeat." You can't delegate your thinking, dreaming or believing to others.

Thomas Edison, who claimed he could think better because of his partial deafness, said, "The best thinking has been done in solitude. The worst has been done in turmoil."

Eagles fly alone; crows fly in groups. Know how to get away and separate yourself. Don't belong so completely to others that you do not belong to yourself. The fact is that we're all in this together–by ourselves.

Alexander Graham Bell made this observation: "Don't keep forever on the public road. Leave the beaten path occasionally and drive into the woods. You'll be certain to find something that you've never seen before. One discovery will lead to another, and before you know it, you will have something worth thinking about to occupy your mind. All really big discoveries are the results of thought." Most big ideas are discovered when you are by yourself.

Don't accept that others know you better than yourself. Great leaders have always encountered noisy opposition from mediocre minds. The biggest mistake that you can make is to believe that others are responsible for your failures and successes. Each of us will give an account of ourselves, not of anyone else, to God.

There is power in the principle of standing alone. More than anyone else, *you* must be persuaded.

The opportunity to succeed or not is yours. No one can take that away unless you let them. Learn to be alone and stand alone, or nothing worthwhile will catch up with you.

Nugget #68

THE LESS YOU ASSOCIATE WITH SOME PEOPLE THE MORE YOUR LIFE WILL IMPROVE.

Who you choose to be your closest friends or associates is one of the most important decisions you will make during the course of your life. "You are the same today that you are going to be in five years from now except for two things: the people with whom you associate and the books you read" (Charlie "Tremendous" Jones). You will become like those you closely associate with.

"Friends in your life are like pillars on your porch: sometimes they hold you up; sometimes they lean on you; sometimes it's just enough to know they're standing by" (Anonymous). A real friend is a person who, when you've made a fool of yourself, lets you forget it. Good friendships always multiply our joy and divide our grief.

Your best friends are those who bring out the best in you. You are better, not worse, after you have been around them.

A good friend never gets in your way unless you're on your way down. They walk in when others walk out. A true friend is someone who is there for you when they'd rather be somewhere else.

The right kind of friends are those with whom you can dare to be yourself, someone you can dream aloud in front of. Sometimes, a single conversation with the right person can be more valuable than many years of study. For me, my best friends are those who understand my past, believe in my future and accept me today just the way I am.

The wrong kind of friends, unlike the good kind of friends, bring out the worst–*not the best*–in you. You know the kind I'm

135

talking about: they are the persons who absorb sunshine and radiate gloom. There are people who will always come up with reasons why you can't do what you want . . . ignore them! It's true what Proverbs says, "Putting confidence in an unreliable man is like chewing with a sore tooth, or trying to run on a broken foot."

A friend is someone who knows all about you but likes you anyway. "Treat your friends as you do your best pictures, and place them in their best light" (Jennie Churchill). A true friend will see you through when others see that you're through. Friends communicate at a heart level. There are good ships and there are bad ships, but the best ships are friendships.

A day away from the wrong associations is like a day in the country. Never have a companion who casts you in the shade. You should have the kind of friends that if you start to thank each other, it would take all day. Mark Twain wrote, "Keep away from people who try to belittle your ambitions. Small people always do that, but the really great make you feel that you, too, can become great."

Nugget #69

IT'S BETTER TO FAIL IN DOING SOMETHING, THAN TO EXCEL IN DOING NOTHING.

Anybody who is currently achieving anything in life is simultaneously risking failure. Failure is often the first necessary step toward success. If we don't risk failing, we won't get the chance to succeed. When we are trying, we are winning. "Never let the fear of striking out get in your way" (Babe Ruth, strike out king, homerun king).

The greatest mistake you can make in life is to be continually fearing you will make one. "Don't be afraid to fail. Don't waste energy trying to cover up failure. If you're not failing, you're not growing," says H. Stanley Judd.

When successful people stop growing and learning it's because they've become less and less willing to risk failure. Failure is delay, not defeat. We all make mistakes–especially those who do things. Only those who don't expect anything, they're the only ones who are never disappointed.

Stop trying to be perfect. When you have a serious decision to make, tell yourself firmly you are going to make it. Don't expect that it will be a perfect one. I love the wisdom of Winston Churchill: "The maxim, 'Nothing avails but perfection,' may be spelled paralysis."

Henry Ward Beecher wrote, "I don't like these cold, precise, perfect people who, in order not to speak wrong, never speak at all, and in order not to do wrong, never do anything." The pursuit of excellence is gratifying and healthy; the pursuit of perfection is frustrating, unproductive and a terrible waste of time.

The fact is that you're like a tea bag. You won't know your own strength until you've been through some hot water. Mistakes

137

are something we can only avoid by saying nothing, doing nothing and being nothing. "Remember, there are two benefits of failure. First, if you do fail, you learn what doesn't work; and second, the failure gives you an opportunity to try a new approach" (Roger Von Oech).

Some defeats are only installments to victory. Henry Ford noted, "Even a mistake may turn out to be the one thing necessary to a worthwhile achievement." Some people learn from their mistakes; some never r cover from them. Learn how to fail intelligently. Develop success from failure.

Mistakes and failure are two of the surest stepping stones to success. "Most people think of success and failure as opposites, but they are actually both products of the same process" (Roger Von Oech). Your season of failure is the best time for sowing your seeds of success.

"No matter what mistakes you have made--no matter how you've messed things up--you can still make a new beginning. The person who fully realizes this suffers less from the shock and pain of failure and sooner gets off to a new beginning," said Norman Vincent Peale.

Successful people are not afraid to fail. They go from failure to failure until at last success is theirs. One of the best ways to accelerate your success is to double your failure rate. The law of failure is one of the most powerful of all success laws.

Nugget #70

WHEN THE WATER STARTS TO RISE, YOU CAN TOO.

To get to the "Promised Land", you'll have to navigate your way through some wilderness. All of us encounter obstacles, problems and challenges. How we respond to them and view them is one of the most important decisions we make. Look at what the book of James says about them: "Dear brothers, is your life full of difficulties and temptations? Then be happy, for when the way is rough, your patience has a chance to grow. So let it grow, and don't try to squirm out of your problems. For when your patience is finally in full bloom, then you will be ready for anything, strong in character, full and complete."

A person with twenty challenges is twice as alive as one with ten. If you haven't got any challenges, you should get down on your knees and ask, "Lord, don't You trust me anymore?" If you've got problems, that's not necessarily bad! Why? Because consistent victories over your problems are steps up the stairway to success. Be thankful for problems, because if they were less difficult, someone with less ability would have your dream.

"A successful man will never see the day that does not bring a fresh quota of problems, and the mark of success is to deal with them effectively" (Lauris Norstad). James Bilkey observed, "You will never be the person you can be if pressure, tension and discipline are taken out of your life." Refuse to let yourself become discouraged by temporary setbacks. If you are beginning to encounter some hard bumps, don't worry. At least you are out of a rut. Circumstances are not your master.

You can always measure a man by the amount of opposition it takes to discourage him. When the water starts to rise, you can too. You can go over, not under. Bernie Siegal wrote, "Obstacles across our path can be spiritual flat tires–disruptions in our lives seem to be disastrous at the time, but end by redirecting our lives in a meaningful way."

The truth is, if you find a path with no obstacles, it is probably a path that doesn't lead to anywhere important. Adversity opens opportunity.

"What is the difference between an obstacle and an opportunity? Our attitude towards it. Every opportunity has a difficulty, and every difficulty has an opportunity," said J. Sidlo Baxter. Lou Holtz says, "Show me someone who has done something worthwhile, and I'll show you someone who has overcome adversity." Many people have good intentions, but then something bad happens and they simply stop. Every path has a puddle, but those puddles can be telling us where to step.

Remember, the travel is worthy of the travail when you're on the right road. If you would just recognize that life is difficult, things would be much easier for you. Norman Vincent Peale pointed out, "Every problem has in it the seeds of its own solution. If you don't have any problems, you don't get any seeds." Look for obstacles. They are your big chance! Live your life so that you can say, "I've had a life full of challenges, thank God!"

Nugget #71

WHEN YOU'RE THROUGH CHANGING, YOU'RE THROUGH.

When you're through changing, you're through. Most people stop growing in life because they're unwilling to make changes.

All mankind is divided into three classes: (1) those who are unchangeable, (2) those who are changeable and (3) those who cause change. "Change is always hardest for the man who is in a rut, for he has scaled down his living to that which he can handle comfortably and welcomes no change or challenge that would lift him up," wrote C. Neil Strait.

If you find yourself in a hole, stop digging. When things go wrong–don't go with them. Stubbornness and unwillingness to change is the strategy of fools.

"He that will not apply new remedies must expect new evils," observed Francis Bacon. Playing it safe is probably the most unsafe thing in the world.

You cannot stand still. You must go forward and be open to those adjustments that improve you. The most unhappy people are those who fear change.

It's been said many times: You can't make an omelet without breaking eggs. Accomplishment automatically results in change. One change makes way for the next, giving us the opportunity to grow. You must change to master change.

You've got to be open to change because every time you think you're ready to graduate from the school of experience, somebody thinks up a new course. Decide to be willing to experience change.

Change but don't stop. Happy is the person who can adjust to a set of circumstances without surrendering his convictions. Open your arms to change, but don't let go of your values.

The majority of people meet with failure because of a lack of persistence in developing new ideas and plans to take place of those which failed. Your growth depends on your willingness to experience change.

You are custom-built for change. You're not a rock. At any point, at any age, any of us can change. Don't let the "way you've always done it" keep you from today's opportunity. When you refuse to change, you end up in chains.

Our Daily Motto Should Be: Give Me The Determination And Tenacity Of A Weed.

A ll great achievements require time and tenacity. Be persevering, because the last key on the ring may be the one that opens the door. Hanging on one second longer than your competition makes you a winner. Become famous for finishing important, difficult tasks.

It's been said that a great oak is only a little nut that held its ground. Too many take hold of opportunity, but let go of it too soon.

Don B. Owens, Jr. said it so well: "Many people fail in life because they believe in the adage: 'If you don't succeed, try something else.' But success eludes those who follow such advice. The dreams that came true did so because people stuck to their ambitions. They refused to be discouraged. They never let disappointment get the upper hand. Challenges only spurred them on to greater efforts."

If you are ever tempted to stop, just think of Brahms, who took seven long years to compose his famous lullaby because he kept falling asleep at the piano (Just kidding. But it did take him seven years to finish). I agree with Woodrow Wilson when he said, "I would rather fail in a cause that will ultimately succeed than succeed in a cause that will ultimately fail." Nearly all failures are the result of people quitting too soon. It takes the hammer of persistence to drive the nail of success.

Many people who fail did not realize how close they were to success when they gave up. Harriet Beecher Stowe wrote, "When you get into a tight place and everything goes against you until it seems as though you could not hold on a minute longer, never give up then, for that is just the time and place that the tide will turn."

The road to success runs uphill, so don't expect to break any speed records. Impatience is costly. Many great mistakes happen because of impatience. Most people fail simply because they're impatient and they cannot join the beginning with the end.

"The determined soul will do more with a rusty monkey wrench than a loafer will accomplish with all the tools in a mechanic's shop," says Rupert Hughs. The power to hold on in spite of everything, to endure--this is the winners quality. To endure is greater than to dare. The difference between the impossible and the possible lies simply in each person's determination.

When you get right down to the root meaning of the word *succeed*, you'll find that it simply means "to persevere and follow through." Any diamond will tell you that it is just a hunk of coal that stuck to its job and made good under pressure.

Nugget #73

WHAT REALLY MATTERS IS WHAT HAPPENS IN US NOT TO US.

L iving a life of unforgiveness is like leaving the parking brake on when you drive your car. It's a drag! It causes you to slow down and lose your momentum. One of the most expensive luxuries that you can possess is unforgiveness toward someone. A deep-seated grudge in your life eats away at your peace of mind like a deadly cancer, destroying a vital organ of life. In fact, there are few things as pathetic to behold as the person who has harbored a grudge and hatred for many years.

If you want to travel far and fast, then travel light. Unpack all of your envies, jealousies, unforgiveness, revenges and fears. Never reject forgiveness or the opportunity to forgive. The weak can never forgive because forgiveness is a characteristic of the strong. Lawrence Sterne said, "Only the brave know how to forgive . . . a coward never forgave; it is not in his nature."

When you live a life of unforgiveness, revenge naturally follows. Revenge is deceptive. It looks sweet, but it's really bitter. It always costs more to avenge a wrong than to bear it. You never can win by trying to even the score.

Be the first to forgive. Forgiveness is your deepest need and highest achievement. Without forgiveness, life is governed by an endless cycle of resentment and retaliation. What a pathetic waste of effort. "He who has not forgiven an enemy has never yet tasted one of the most sublime enjoyments of life,"declares Johann Lavater. Forgiveness is the key to personal peace. Forgiveness releases you and creates freedom.

One of the secrets of a long and fruitful life is to forgive everybody everything every night before you go to bed.

Forgiving those who have wronged you is a key to personal peace. Peter Von Winter said, "It is manlike to punish, but Godlike to forgive." When you have a huge chip on your shoulder, it causes you to lose your balance. When you stop nursing a grudge, it dies. Forgiveness is a funny thing. It warms the heart and cools the sting.

It is far better to forgive and forget than to hate and remember. Josh Billings says, "There is no revenge so complete as forgiveness." Richard Nixon said, "Those who hate you don't win unless you hate them, and then you destroy yourself." This is a fact: unforgiveness blocks blessings, forgiveness releases blessings.

Do you want to release the past and claim the future? Get a hold of what Paul Boese said, "Forgiveness does not change the past, but it does enlarge the future." You can be wrong in the middle of being right when you don't forgive someone. "Protest long enough that you are right and you will be wrong" (Yiddish proverb).

Don't burn bridges. You'll be surprised how many times you have to cross over that same river. Unforgiveness is empty, but forgiveness makes a future possible. You'll "start your day on the right foot" if you ask yourself everyday, "Who do I need to forgive?"

Nugget #74

UNLESS YOU ENTER THE BEEHIVE, YOU CAN'T TAKE THE HONEY.

"Shoot for the moon. Even if you miss it, you will land among the stars" (Les Brown). You and I are like rubber bands. We are most useful when we are stretched.

You can only accomplish in proportion to what you attempt. The reason so little is accomplished is generally because so little is attempted.

"It is not because things are difficult that we do not dare; it is because we do not dare that things are difficult" (Seneca). The definition of impossible: something nobody can do until somebody does. Never say never. You have to think big to be big.

The fact is, it's fun to do the impossible. When we're playing it safe, we create the most insecurity. So, look at things . . . as they can be.

You do not tap the talents inside of you until you attempt the impossible. Risk is part of every success plan. "Mediocre minds usually dismiss anything which reaches beyond their own understanding" (Rochfoucauld).

Calvin Coolidge said, "We do not need more intellectual power, we need more spiritual power. We do not need more things that are seen, we need more of the things that are unseen." The book of Philippians says, "I can do everything God asks me to with the help of Christ who gives me the strength and power."

Look for ways to exercise your risk muscle. Everyone has a risk muscle, and you keep it in the proper shape by experimenting and trying new things. Bite off more than you can chew.

"People who take risks are the people you'll lose against" (John Scully). "The people who are really failures are the people who set their standards so low, keep the bar at such a safe level, that they never run the risk of failure" (Robert Schuller).

A great ship always asks for deep water. When you dare for nothing you should hope for nothing. Progress always involves risk. You can't steal second base and keep your foot on first. He who does not dare will not get his share.

Nugget #75

BEFORE LOOKING FOR A WAY TO GET, LOOK FOR A WAY TO GIVE.

"Nobody cares how much you know until they know how much you care" (John Cassis). Life is a lot like the game of tennis. Those who don't serve well end up losing.

A man asked Dr. Carl Menninger, "What would you advise a person to do if he felt a nervous breakdown coming on?" Most people expected him to reply, "Consult a psychiatrist." To their astonishment he replied, "Lock up your house, go across the railroad tracks, find someone in need and do something to help that person."

"Unless life is lived for others, it is not worthwhile. A self-centered life is totally empty" (Mother Teresa). If you are dissatisfied with your lot in life, build a *service* station on it. A good way to forget your troubles is to help others out of theirs.

Serving others is never entirely unselfish, because the giver always receives. Proverbs says, "Your own soul is nourished when you are kind; it is destroyed when you are cruel." Think about what questions you will be asked at the close of your life on earth. Nathan Schaeffer says, "The question will not be, 'How much have you got?' but, 'How much have you given?' Not, 'How much have you won' but 'How much have you done?' Not, 'How much have you saved' but 'How much have you sacrificed?' It will be, 'How much have you loved and served?' not, 'How much were you honored?'"

"Selfishness is the greatest curse of the human race" (W. E. Gladstone). Self-interest is a fire that consumes others and then itself.

Almost all of our unhappiness is the result of selfishness. Instead, think in terms of what the other person wants, not just what you want. It is absolutely true that you can succeed best and quickest by helping others succeed.

"The measure of life is not in its duration, but in its donation. Everyone can be great because everyone can serve" (Peter Marshall). When you are serving others, life is no longer meaningless.

"One thing I know; the only ones among you who will really be happy are those who have sought and found how to serve" (Albert Schweitzer). You can't help another without helping yourself.

No one achieves greatness without being of service. Never reach out your hand unless you're willing to extend an arm and your heart. The roots of happiness grow deepest in the soil of service. Happiness is like potato salad—when shared with others, it's a picnic.

COMPARISON IS NEVER PROOF OF ANYTHING.

"Every man must do two things alone," said Martin Luther. "He must do his own believing and his own dying." When you compare yourself with others, you will become bitter or vain because there will always be people better or worse than you.

Making comparisons is a sure path to frustration. "You can't clear your own fields while counting the rocks on your neighbor's farm" (Joan Welch). "The grass may be greener on the other side of the fence, but there's probably more of it to mow" (Lois Cory). Hills look small and green a long way off.

It's a waste of time and energy when you compare your life to that of other people. Life is more fun when you don't keep your score against others. Success really is simply a matter of doing what you do best and not worrying about what the other person is going to do.

You carry success or failure within yourself. It does not depend on outside conditions. Success in someone else's life does not hurt the chances for success in yours.

Ask yourself this question that Earl Nightingale posed: "Are you motivated by what you really want out of life, or are you mass-motivated?" Make sure you decide what you really want, not what someone else wants for you. Do you say, "I'm good, but not as good as I ought to be," or do you compare and say, "I'm not as bad as a lot of other people?"

The longer you dwell on another's weakness, the more you affect your own mind with unhappiness. You must create your own system and your own plan, or someone else's will limit you.

What happens in an other person's life, good or bad, has nothing to do with how you are doing in your own life. If I compare myself to John Grisham, I'll never write another book, but if I compare myself to Adolf Hitler, I'll think I'm a saint.

Don't think you're necessarily on the right road because it's a well-beaten path. The greatest risk in life is to wait for and depend on others for your security and satisfaction. Don't measure yourself with another man's coat. Don't judge yourself through someone else's eyes.

LIFT PEOPLE UP, DON'T PUT THEM DOWN.

One of the most exciting decisions you can make is to be on the lookout for opportunities to invest in others. For me, this has been one of the most powerful principles of momentum I've implemented in my life. About ten years ago, I remember driving to Tulsa, Oklahoma, from St. Louis, Missouri with my family. I was listening to a Zig Ziglar tape and on this tape he said, "You'll always have everything you want in life if you'll help enough other people get what they want." When I heard this statement, literally, something went off inside of me, and I said out loud, "I'm going to do it." That decision to look for ways to help others, to invest in them, changed my life.

I believe that one of the marks of true greatness is to develop greatness in others. "There are three keys to more abundant living: caring about others, daring for others and sharing with others" (William Ward).

I have found that really great men have a unique perspective. That perspective is that greatness is not deposited in them to stay but rather to flow through them into others. "We make a living by what we get, but we make a life by what we give" (Norman MacEwan). Assign yourself the purpose of making others happy and successful.

People have a way of becoming what you encourage them to be. Ralph Waldo Emerson observed, "Trust men and they will be true to you; treat them greatly and they will show themselves great." Goethe advised, "Treat people as if they were what they ought to be and help them to become what they are capable of being.

Whatever we praise, we increase. There is no investment you can make that will pay you so well as investing in the

· improvement of others throughout your life. "The person who renders loyal service in a humble capacity will be chosen for higher responsibilities, just as the biblical servant who multiplied the one pound given by his master was made ruler over ten cities" (B. C. Forbes).

There are two types of people in the world: those who come into a room and say, "Here I am!" and those who come in and say, "Ah, there you are!" How do you know a good person? A good person makes others good. Find happiness by helping others find it.

A good deed bears interest. You cannot hold a light to another's path without brightening your own. Develop greatness in others.

"There is no more noble occupation in the world than to assist another human being—to help someone succeed" (Allan McGinnis). "The true meaning of life is to plant trees under whose shade you do not expect to sit" (Nelson Henderson). The greatest use of your life is to spend it for something and on someone that will outlast it. "If you cannot win, make the one ahead of you break the record" (Jan McKeithen). Invest in others. It pays great dividends.

Nugget #78

WHO GIVES YOU MORE TROUBLE THAN YOU?

Here's the first rule of winning: don't beat yourself. Your biggest enemy is you. Have you felt like Dwight L. Moody when he said, "I have never met a man who has given me as much trouble as myself"? The first and best victory is to conquer yourself.

Very often a change of self is needed more than a change of scenery. Only you can hold yourself back. There is no one to stop you but yourself.

Talk back to your internal critic. "If you want to move your greatest obstacle, realize that your obstacle is yourself–and that the time to act is now" (Nido Cubein).

You must begin to think of yourself as becoming the person you want to be. "Give the man you'd like to be a look at the man you are" (Edgar Guest). Change what you tell yourself. "No one really knows enough to be a pessimist" (Norman Cousins).

Remember, "One of the nice things about problems is that a good many of them do not exist except in our imaginations" (Steve Allen). The fear you fear is only in yourself and nowhere else.

Most of the important battles we face will be waged within ourselves. There are two forces warring against each other inside us. One says, "You can't!"; the other says, "You can!" Be encouraged by this fact found in the book of Matthew, "With God all things are possible."

The basic problem most people have is that they are doing nothing to solve their basic problem. This problem is: they build a case against themselves. They are their own worst enemy.

All of what we are, good and bad, is what we have thought and believed. So, don't put water in your own boat, the storm will put enough in on its own. Don't dream up thousands of reasons why you can't do what you want to; find one reason why you can. It is easier to do all the things you should do than spend the rest of your life wishing you had.

We lie loudest when we lie to ourselves. "You can't consistently perform in a manner that is inconsistent with the way you see yourself," says Zig Ziglar. Determine to multiply your commitment, divide your distractions, subtract your excuses and add your faith. The first key victory you must win is over yourself.

Nugget #79

THINK THANKS.

Be aggressively thankful. When it comes to living, do you take things for granted or take them with gratitude? Thanksgiving is the attitude of a productive life.

No duty is more urgent than that of returning thanks. How long has it been since you thanked those closest to you? The person who isn't thankful for what he's got isn't likely to be thankful for what he's going to get. Ingratitude never ends.

"Attitudes sour in the life that is closed to thankfulness. Soon selfish attitudes take over, closing life to better things" (C. Neil Strait). The person who forgets the language of gratitude will never find themselves on speaking terms with happiness.

Thanksgiving, you will find, creates power in your life because it opens the generators of your heart to respond gratefully, to receive joyfully and to react creatively. William Ward spoke wisely: "There are three enemies of personal peace: regret over yesterday's mistakes, anxiety over tomorrow's problems and ingratitude for today's blessing."

We all have a lot to be thankful for. For example: No matter what house you live in, wouldn't you rather be there than the best hospital in your city? If you can't be satisfied with what you've reached, be thankful for what you've escaped.

Count your blessings at every opportunity. Take some time today to reflect on all you have to be thankful for. The words *think* and *thank* come from the same Latin root. If we take time to *think* more, we will undoubtedly *thank* more.

I like what Dwight L. Moody said: "Be humble or you'll stumble." There's an inescapable relationship between pride and ingratitude. Henry Ward Beecher pointed out, "A proud man is seldom a grateful man, for he never thinks he gets as much as he deserves."

Don't be a person who has a highly developed instinct for being unhappy. The best rule is: whatever you are given, gratefully receive it. When you spend your time thanking others for the good things, there won't be any time left to complain about the bad.

Find fifty things to be thankful for today. As you do, creative ideas will spring forth as a result of the mental conversation you are having with yourself. One of the best ways to generate momentum and opportunities is to sit down and write a thank-you note to people who have influenced your life.

The most highly satisfied life can be found in being thankful. Appreciative words are one of the most powerful forces for good on the earth. Thankful words don't cost much, yet they accomplish so much. So, count your blessings; don't discount them.

Nugget #80

THERE'S NO EXCUSE FOR BEING FULL OF EXCUSES.

"Ninety-nine percent of failures come from people who have a habit of making excuses" (George Washington Carver). You are never a failure until you begin to blame somebody else. Stop blaming others. You'll find that when you become good at making excuses you won't be good at anything else. Excuses are the tools a person with no purpose or vision uses to build great monuments of emptiness.

You can learn from your mistakes if you don't waste your time denying and defending them. "It seems to me these days that people who admit they're wrong get a lot further than people who prove they're right" (Deryl Pfizer). What poison is to food, alibis are to a productive life. "Work brings profit; talk brings poverty" (Proverbs). "Some men have thousands of reasons why they cannot do what they want to do when all they really need is one reason why they can" (Willis Whitney).

One of the biggest alibis is regret. Don't leave any regrets on the field–give your all in the game of life. "The most valuable thing I have learned from life is to regret nothing" (Somerset Maugham). Eliminate all your regrets. "Regret is an appalling waste of energy; you can't build on it. It's only good for wallowing in" (Catherine Mansfield). The truth is, a thousand regrets do not pay one debt. Live your life so that your tombstone reads, "No regrets."

When a winner makes a mistake, he says, "I was wrong." When a loser makes a mistake, he says, "It wasn't my fault." Do you admit and say, "I was wrong," or do you say, "It wasn't my fault?" A winner explains; a loser explains away.

Idle people lack no excuses. The word *can't* usually means you won't try. The word *can't* weakens our resolve and many times does more harm than slander or lies. *Can't* is the worst excuse and the foremost enemy of success.

We have many reasons for failure but not a real excuse. "Excuses always replace progress" (Ralph Waldo Emerson). The book of Philippians says it best: "In everything you do, stay away from complaining and arguing, so that no one can speak a word of blame against you." Alibis and excuses should be cremated, not embalmed. The person who excuses himself always accuses himself. Denying a fault doubles it.

"The best years of your life are the ones in which you decide your problems are your own. You don't blame them on your mother, the ecology or the president. You realize that you control your own destiny" (Albert Ellis). Don't buy that alibi. We should live our lives like Florence Nightingale when she said, "I attribute my success to this: I never gave or took an excuse."

Nugget #81

BROKEN PROMISES CAUSE THE WORLD'S GREATEST ACCIDENTS.

You can't make wrong work. Thomas Jefferson said, "Honesty is the first chapter of the book of wisdom." Never chase a lie: if you leave it alone, it will run itself to death. Everything you add to the truth, you inevitably subtract from it. It's discouraging to think how people nowadays are more shocked by honesty than by deceit.

"Those that think it is permissible to tell 'white lies' soon grow colorblind" (Awson O'Malley). We punish ourselves with every lie and we reward ourselves with every right action. A lie will add to your troubles, subtract from your energy, multiply your difficulties and divide your effectiveness.

"Truth is always strong, no matter how weak it looks, and falsehood is always weak no matter how strong it looks" (Marcus Antonius). Never view anything positively that makes you break your word. Make your word your bond.

In the war between falsehood and truth, falsehood wins the first battle, but truth wins the war. "If we live truly, we shall truly live," said Ralph Waldo Emerson. Liars are never free. Horace Greeley observed, "The darkest hour of any man's life is when he sits down to plan how to get money without earning it."

The book of Proverbs says it best: "Dishonest gain will never last, so why take the risk?" Honesty always lasts longest. A lie never lives to be old.

"It makes all the difference in the world whether we put truth in the first place or in the second place" (John Morley). As scarce as the truth is, the supply has always been in excess of the demand. Wrong is wrong no matter who does it or says it. Truth does not cease to exist because it is ignored, and it doesn't

161

change depending on whether it is believed by a majority of people. The truth is always the strongest argument.

Truth exists. Only lies are created. Truth shines in darkness. "There is never an instant's truth between virtue and vice. Goodness is the only investment that never fails" (Henry David Thoreau). Truth needs no crutches. If it limps, it's a lie. "You'll find that life is an uphill battle for the person who's not on the level" (Joan Welsh).

"If you continue to do what's right, what's wrong and who's wrong will eventually leave your life" (David Blunt). A businessman had personalized letterhead that read, "Right is right even if everyone is against it, and wrong is wrong even if everyone is for it."

Consider the words of John Wesley:

Do all the good you can, In all the ways you can,

In all the places you can, At all times you can,

To all the people you can, As long as ever you can.

DON'T STRIKE WHEN THE IRON IS COLD.

Don't be a person who says, "Ready! Aim, aim, aim, aim." As fast as each opportunity presents itself, seize it! No matter how small the opportunity may be, use it!

Do what you need to do when it ought to be done whether you like it or not. "He who hesitates misses the green light, gets bumped in the rear, and loses his parking space" (Herbert Prochnow).

One of the deceptive beliefs of those who live an unproductive life is that today is not an important day. Every day comes to us bearing gifts. Untie its bow, tear into the wrapping, open it up. Write on your heart every day that it is the best day of the year.

By the time the hesitant person has learned to play the game, the players have dispersed, and the rules have changed. Don't find yourself striking when the iron is cold. Instead, scratch opportunity when and where it itches. Life is made up of constant calls to action.

"Successful leaders have the courage to take action while others hesitate" (John Maxwell). You will never know what you can do until you begin. Remember, the moment you say, "I give up," someone else is seeing the same situation and saying, "My, what a great opportunity."

No opportunity is ever lost; someone else picks up those that are missed. One secret of success in life is to be ready for opportunity when it comes. Ability is empty apart from opportunity.

Time flies. It's up to you to be the pilot. "Everything comes to him who hustles while he waits" (Thomas Edison). It has been my observation that productive people get ahead during the time that others waste. Make quick use of the moment.

It is later than you think. Be ready now. Life's alarm clock has no snooze button. It doesn't do any good to "stand up and take notice" if you sit down as soon as opportunity passes by. Look at it, size it up, make a decision. You postpone your life when you can't make up your mind.

William Ward has this recipe for success: "Study while others are sleeping; work while others are loafing; prepare while others are playing and dream while others are wishing." There is no time like the present and no present like time. Those who take advantage of their advantage get the advantage in this world. Don't find yourself at the end of your life saying, "What a wonderful life I've had! I only wish I realized it sooner."

Nugget #83

WHEN YOU RUN IN PLACE, EVERYONE WILL PASS YOU BY.

Failure's most successful strategy is procrastination. *Now* is the best time to be alive and productive. If you want to make an easy job seem difficult, just keep putting off doing it. "We're all fugitives, and the things we didn't do yesterday are the bloodhounds" (Prism). Said Joseph Newton, "A duty dodged is like a debt unpaid; it is only deferred and we must come back and settle the account at last."

What holds people back? "There are those of us who are always 'about' to live. We're waiting until things change, until there is more time, until we are less tired, until we get a promotion, until we settle down–until, until, until. It always seems that there is some major event that must occur in our lives before we begin living" (George Sheehan). *One* of these days is really *none* of these days. The "sweet by and by" never comes. People who desire, but don't act, soon find themselves frozen. They make as much progress as a glacier.

About the only thing that comes to a procrastinator is old age. Do today what you want to postpone until tomorrow. "Do not allow idleness to deceive you; for while you give him today, he steals tomorrow from you" (H. Crowquill). Nothing is so fatiguing as the eternal hanging-on of an uncompleted task.

When a person gets into a habit of wasting time, they are sure to waste a great deal that does not belong to them. "One day, today, is worth two tomorrows" (Ben Franklin). What may be done at any time will be done at no time. "Life is like a taxi, the meter keeps a-ticking whether you're getting somewhere or standing still" (Lou Erickson). The successful person does the thing that others never get around to. What the fool does in the end, the wise person does in the beginning.

"Don't stand shivering upon the banks; plunge in at once and have it over with" (Sam Slick). Tomorrow is the busiest day of the week. If there's a hill to climb, don't think that waiting will make it any smaller.

An unsuccessful person takes a hundred steps because they would not take one at the right time. If possible, make the decision now, even if the action is in the future. A reviewed decision is usually better than one reached at the last moment. "The fool with all his other thoughts, has this also: he is always getting ready to live" (Epicurus). He who fiddles around seldom gets to lead the orchestra. There is danger in delay because it is always better to reap two days too soon than one day too late.

Attack procrastination by eliminating all excuses and reasons for not taking decisive and immediate action. "Tomorrow will I live," the fool does say; tomorrow itself is too late; the wise live yesterday" (Martial). "While the fool is enjoying the little he has, I will hunt for more. The way to hunt for more is to utilize your odd moments . . . the man who is always killing time is really killing his own chances in life" (Arthur Brisbane).

THERE'S ALWAYS A HEAVY DEMAND FOR FRESH MEDIOCRITY– DON'T GIVE IN TO IT.

S tart every task thinking how to do it better than it has ever been done before. "Start a crusade in your life to dare to be your very best" (William Danforth). Become a yardstick of quality. Do the right thing regardless of what others think.

"It is a funny thing about life; if you refuse to accept anything but the best, you very often get it" (Somerset Maugham). Think only of the best, work only for the best and expect only the best. Excellence is never an accident. "There is a way to do it better . . . find it" (Thomas Edison).

There's always an excellent way of doing everything. "Hold yourself responsible for a higher standard than anybody else expects of you. Never excuse yourself" (Henry Ward Beecher). Most people aren't used to an environment where excellence is expected.

"It is those who have this imperative demand for the best in their natures and those who will accept nothing short of it, that hold the banners of progress, that set the standards, the ideals for others" (Orsen Marden).

Excellence measures a man by the height of his ideals, the breadth of his compassion, the depth of his convictions and the length of his persistence. People will always determine your character by observing what you stand for or fall for.

Don't seek success. Instead, seek excellence, and you will find both. Work to become, not to acquire. Do the very best you can, and leave the results to take care of themselves. People are funny; they spend money they don't have, to buy things they don't need, to impress people they don't like. Success is not found in achieving what you aim at but in aiming at what you ought to achieve.

Perfection, fortunately, is not the best alternative to mediocrity. A more sensible alternative is excellence. Striving for excellence rather than perfection is stimulating and rewarding; striving for perfection in practically anything is frustrating and futile.

We are what we repeatedly do. Excellence, then, is not an act but a habit. "Excellence demands that you be better than yourself" (Ted Engstrom).

Be easily satisfied with the very best. When you are delivering your very best is when you will feel most successful. Never sell your principles for popularity or you'll find yourself bankrupt in the worst way. Dare to be true to the best you know.

LIFE'S MOST IMPORTANT ANSWERS CAN BE FOUND IN ASKING THE RIGHT QUESTIONS.

Do you tackle problems bigger than you?

Do you leave others better than you found them?

Is your favorite letter "I"?

Do you believe your doubts and doubt your beliefs?

What would happen if you changed the words you spoke about your biggest problem? Your biggest opportunity?

Are you becoming ordinary?

Will people say this about your life?: "He did nothing in particular and he did it very well."

How much of you does your dream have?

Is it a long way from your words to your deeds?

If you try to be like him (or her), who will be like you?

Do you give up control of your life to something other than what you believe?

What kind of world would this be if everyone were just like you?

If you don't take action now, what will this ultimately cost you?

Are you a person who says, "My decision is maybe–and that's final!"?

Are you making dust or eating dust? (Bill Grant)

Do you count your blessings or think your blessings don't count?

Do you need a good swift kick in the seat of your "can'ts"?

Are you known by the promises you don't keep?

Would the boy you were be proud of the man you are?

Are you already disappointed with the future?

Nugget #86

An Original Is Hard To Find But Easy To Recognize.

How many outstanding people do you know with unique and distinctive characteristics? They're *different*. I believe that one of the greatest compliments you can receive is for someone to come up to you and say, "You're different!" I'm not suggesting that you be weird for weirdness' sake. Be yourself, and you will stand out.

Don't be a living custard. It's true what Eric Hoffer said: "When people are free to do as they please, they usually imitate each other." Man is the only creation that refuses to be what he is.

Don't be awestruck by other people and try to copy them. Nobody can be you as efficiently and as effectively as you can. One of the hardest things about climbing the ladder of success is getting through the crowd of copies at the bottom.

The number of people who don't take advantage of their talents is more than made up for by the number who take advantage of the talents they scarcely have. Begin to accept the way God made you.

You are a specialist. You are not created to be all things to all people. More than 90 percent of all flowers have either an unpleasant odor or none at all. Yet it is the ones with sweet fragrance that we most remember. Stand out!

"Following the path of least resistance is what makes men and rivers crooked," says Larry Bielat. Too many people make cemeteries of their lives by burying their talents and gifts. These abilities are like deposits in our personal accounts, and we get to determine the interest. The more interest and attention we give them, the more valuable they become.

The copy adapts himself to the world, but the original tries to adapt the world to him. It doesn't take a majority to make a change—it takes only a few determined originals and a sound cause. I agree with the old saying that said, "You're the only one in all of creation who has your set of abilities. You're special . . . you're rare. And in all rarity there is great worth."

"Could Hamlet have been written by a committee, or the Mona Lisa painted by a club? Could the New Testament have been composed as a conference report? Creative ideas do not spring from groups. They spring from individuals," said A. Whitney Griswold.

Each of us has our own unique, individual way. There are no precedents; you are the first *you* that ever was. You are the most qualified person on the face of the earth to do what you are destined to do.

Nugget #87

OPPORTUNITIES HIDE BEHIND OBSTACLES.

Not all obstacles are bad. In fact, an opportunity's favorite disguise is an obstacle. You will always meet obstacles on the road to your answer. The fight is good; it is proof that you haven't quit and are still alive.

No one is immune to problems. Even the lion has to fight off flies. The apostle Paul said it best when he wrote, "We are pressed on every side by troubles, but not crushed, and broken. We are perplexed because we don't know why things happen as they do, but we don't give up and quit. We get knocked down, but we get up again and keep going."

Being a diligent person does not remove you from the world and its problems; rather, it positions you to live in it productively and victoriously. Thomas Carlyle said, "The block of granite which was an obstacle in the pathway of the weak becomes a stepping-stone in the pathway of the strong."

Good news for you! In the midst of every trial, there is growth and promotion for you. Each challenge provides an opportunity to grow, not die.

Obstacles can temporarily detour you, but only *you* can make *you* stop. Your struggle may be lasting, but it is not everlasting. It's wrong to think that there's nothing more permanent than this temporary situation.

Obstacles will reveal what you truly believe and who you really are. They introduce you to yourself. You will find out what you honestly believe in the face of a problem.

As I've traveled, I've always noticed that no matter how cloudy it is when the plane takes off, above the clouds the sun always shines. Look up! It's not the "out look" but the "up look" that counts.

Your life will be much more productive if you just understand that obstacles are a part of life. If you want your place in the sun, you'll have to expect some blisters. Studs Terkel said, "Face the music and someday you may lead the band." The difference between iron and steel is fire, but the fire-tried steel is worth it.

It's Not What You Have; It's What You Do With What You Have.

Few dreams come true by themselves. The test of a person lies in action. No one ever stumbled onto something big while sitting down. Thomas Edison said it best, "Opportunity is missed by most people because it is dressed in overalls and looks like work."

Even a mosquito doesn't get a slap on the back until he starts to work. A famous anonymous poem states, "Sitting still and wishing makes no person great; the good Lord sends the fishing, but you must dig the bait."

Nothing is learned while you talk. Words without actions are the assassins of dreams. The smallest good deed produces more than the greatest intention.

History is made whenever you take the right action. Action is the proper fruit of knowledge. You earn respect only by action; inaction earns disrespect.

You'll find life an empty dream if you put nothing into it. Every time one person expresses an idea, he finds ten others who thought of it before–but took no action. Ideas times nothing equals nothing. It takes work.

The longer you only talk about an idea, the less likely you are to actually do it. One sure way to wear out a friendship is to continually talk about your "big" idea. It's time to put feet to your dream!

Mark Twain said, "Thunder is good, thunder is impressive, but it is lightning that does the work." Gold is of no value until it is worked and mined out of the ground. The test of this book is not that the reader goes away saying, "What an interesting and informative book," but rather saying, "I will do something!"

Getting an idea should be like sitting on a tack—it should make you jump up and do something. George Bernard Shaw said, "When I was young, I observed that nine out of every ten things I did were failures. So I did ten times more work." Too many people avoid discovering the secret of success because deep down they suspect the secret may be hard work.

Nugget #89

IF AT FIRST YOU DO SUCCEED, TRY SOMETHING HARDER.

All progress is due to those who were not satisfied to let well enough alone. "Acorns were good until bread was found," said Sir Francis Bacon. The majority of men fail because of their lack of persistence in creating new plans to improve those that succeed.

If you can't think up a new idea, find a way to make better use of an old one. "Where we cannot invent, we may at least improve," said Charles Caleb Colton.

Don't look for the answer to your problem; look for many answers, then choose the best one. Do more than is required and continue doing it. "The difference between ordinary and extraordinary is that little extra," says Zig Ziglar.

There is always a way–then there is always a better way. When you've found something–look again. School is never out! The more you truly desire something, the more you will try to find a better way.

The biggest enemy of best is good. If you're satisfied with what's good, you'll never have what's best. "It's what you learn after you know it all that counts," says John Wooden.

The man who thinks he knows it all has merely stopped thinking. If you think you've arrived, you'll be left behind. A successful man continues to look for work after he has found a job.

Take the offensive. Cause something to happen. Don't waste time defending your present position. Create a habit of taking the initiative and don't ever start your day in neutral. Don't leave well enough alone.

"Show me a thoroughly satisfied man, and I will show you a failure," said Thomas Edison. "There are two kinds of men who never amount to very much," Cyrus H.K. Curtis remarked to his associate, Edward Bok. "And what kinds are those?" inquired Bok. "Those who cannot do what they are told," replied the famous publisher, "and those who can do nothing else." Find a better way, and make that way better.

Nugget #90

THE WAY TO ELIMINATE CRITICISM: DO NOTHING AND BE NOTHING.

All great ideas create conflict. In other words, what you want to do in life will create challenges and criticism. Decide today: I will not surrender my dream to noisy negatives.

Every great idea has this order of responses:

1. "It is impossible–don't waste the time and the money."

2. "It is possible but has a limited value."

3. "I said it was a good idea all along."

Foes and critics are never interested in solving the problem, and they never offer a better solution. They are like an armless man who teaches throwing.

If your head sticks up above the crowd, expect more criticism than applause. Have you ever noticed that a statue has never been erected to a critic?

Whoever criticizes to you will criticize about you. If someone belittles you, he is only trying to cut you down to his size. While throwing mud, critics are simultaneously losing ground.

You can always tell a failure by the way he criticizes success. Those who can–do. Those who can't–criticize. Those who complain about the way the ball bounces are usually the ones who dropped it.

If it were not for the doers, the critics would soon be out of business. Envy provides the mud that failures throw at success. Kenneth Tynan put it this way, "A critic is a man who thinks he knows the way, but can't drive the car." Small minds are the first to condemn great ideas.

If people talk negatively about you, live and work so that no one will believe them. Fear of criticism is the kiss of death in the courtship of achievement.

If you are afraid of criticism, you won't accomplish much. A successful man is one who can lay a firm foundation with the bricks that others throw at him.

DON'T TRY TO GET EVEN WITH YOUR ENEMIES AND AHEAD OF YOUR FRIENDS.

Picture a runner in full stride. He speeds through a pack of contenders, but he begins to look at whom he's running against. What is the inevitable conclusion to this scene? That runner will slow down and probably stumble. The same will happen to us if we allow the distraction of envy to turn our head as we run the race set before us. Instead of breaking records, we're breaking our momentum.

"The man who covets is always poor" (Claudian). Envy never enriched any man. "Of all the passions, jealousy is that which exacts the hardest service and pays the bitterest wages. Its service is to watch the success of our enemy; its wages, to be sure of it" (Charles Colton).

Envy is like biting a dog because the dog bit you. Here's an accurate description: "Envy shoots at others and wounds herself" (English proverb). It is self-punishment. "A relaxed attitude lengthens a man's life; jealousy rots it away" (Proverbs). Like rust consumes iron, envy consumes itself.

Envy drains the joy, satisfaction, and purpose out of living. If allowed to grow, it breeds hate and revenge. Revenge converts a little right into a big wrong. Watch out! It is an appetite that is never satisfied.

"It is not love that is blind, but jealousy" (Lawrence Durrell). Envy sees the sea but not the rocks. "When an envious man hears another praised, he feels himself injured" (English proverb).

"Love looks through a telescope, envy through a microscope" (Josh Billings). We underrate or exaggerate that which we don't possess. Your life is too valuable to waste by wanting what others have.

Some people seem to know how to live everybody's lives but their own. Envy is the consuming desire to have everybody else a little less successful than you are. Don't measure your success by what others have or haven't done.

Envy is a tremendous waste of mental energy. Refrain from it—it will be the root of most of your unhappiness. Jealously is the tribute mediocrity pays to achievers.

A person is wise when they don't long for the things that they don't have, but is thankful for those things that they do have. Continually compare what you want with what you have, and you'll be unhappy. Instead, compare what you deserve with what you have, and you'll be happy. Decide to stick with appreciation. Envy is too great a burden to bear.

Nugget #92

SUCCESS HAS MADE FAILURES OF MANY PEOPLE.

How many people of great potential have you known? Where did they all go? If people of great potential stop it's because they don't build on their victories. There are two distinct times when a person is most likely to quit; after a mistake or after a victory.

Once you're moving you can keep moving. Does Michael Jordan stop shooting after making his first basket? Did John Grisham quit writing after his first best-seller? Successful people know that each victory buys an admission ticket to a more challenging opportunity.

One of the greatest benefits of success is the opportunity to do more. "Opportunities multiply as they are seized" (John Wicker). The more you do, the more you can do.

"Perhaps it is a good thing that you haven't seen all your dreams come true. For when you get all you wish for, you will be miserable. To be forever reaching out, to remain unsatisfied is a key to momentum" (*North Carolina Christian Advocate*). I'm not suggesting that you don't stop and smell the roses along the journey. Just don't stay so long past the victory of the blossom that the petals have dropped, the limbs have been pruned and all that's left is the thorns.

The first step towards going somewhere significant is to decide that you are not going to stay where you are. When you have a victory, comfort and money will come but don't confuse comfort with happiness and money with success.

It's not what you get that makes you successful; rather, it is what you are continuing to do with what you've got that's a better yardstick. The person who is satisfied with what he has done will never become famous for what he will do.

Remember this your lifetime through—

Tomorrow, there will be more to do

And failure waits for all those who stay

With some success made yesterday.

(Anonymous)

BE LIKE THE MONA LISA; SHE KEEPS SMILING WHEN HER BACK'S TO THE WALL.

Enthusiasm makes everything different. You can't control the length of each day, but you can control its impact by adding fun and enthusiasm. When you have enthusiasm for life, life has enthusiasm for you.

William Ward said, "Enthusiasm and persistence can make an average person superior; indifference and lethargy can make a superior person average." Don't postpone joy.

If you find yourself dog-tired at night, it may be because you growled all day. Learn to laugh at yourself. A person with a great sense of humor may bore others, but he rarely has a dull moment himself.

Enthusiasm is an inside job. "Of all the things God created, I am often most grateful He created laughter" (Chuck Swindoll). Humor is to life what shock absorbers are to automobiles. Thank God for them on bumpy roads!

One of the single most powerful things you can do to have influence over others is to smile at them. You are never fully dressed until you wear a smile. The best facelift is a smile.

A smile is an asset; a frown is a liability. Some people grin and bear it; others smile and change it. Smiling–being happy and enthusiastic–is always a choice, not a result. It improves your personality and peoples' opinion of you.

Both enthusiasm and pessimism are contagious. How much of each do you spread? Our attitudes tell others what we expect in return. "It's difficult to remain neutral or indifferent in the presence of a positive thinker" (Denis Waitley). A laugh a day keeps negative people away.

You can succeed at almost anything for which you have unlimited enthusiasm. "In my experience, the best creative work is never done when one is unhappy," said Albert Einstein.

Enthusiasm gives you the proper perspective on life. Helen Keller said, "Keep your face to the sunshine and you cannot see the shadow." A smile is a powerful, positive weapon by which to attack life.

Every significant success is accomplished with enthusiasm. For every opportunity you miss because you're too enthusiastic, you will miss a hundred because you're not enthusiastic enough. You will rarely succeed at anything unless you have fun doing it.

"WINNING STARTS WITH BEGINNINGS" (ROBERT SCHULLER)

Everything big starts with something little. Nothing great is created suddenly. Nothing can be done except little by little. Never decide to do nothing just because you can only do a little.

People who think they are too big to do little things are perhaps too little to be asked to do big things. Small opportunities are often the beginning of great enterprises.

Within a little thing lies a big opportunity. Small things make a big difference; therefore, do all that it takes to be successful in little things.

One of the most frequent prayers I pray is, "Lord send small opportunities into my life." I know that if I am faithful in the small things, bigger opportunities open up to me.

You will never do great things if you can't do small things in a great way. All difficult things have their beginning in that which is easy, and great things in that which is small.

One of the major differences between people who have momentum and those who don't is that those with momentum are growing by taking advantage of small opportunities. The impossible, many times, is simply the untried. Here's some of the best advice I've been given: "Do something!"

The courage to begin is the same courage it takes to succeed. This is the courage that usually separates dreamers from achievers.

The beginning is the most important part of any endeavor. Worse than a quitter is anyone who is afraid to begin. Ninety percent of success is showing up and starting. You may be disappointed if you fail, but you are doomed if you don't try.

Don't be deceived; knowledge alone of where you want to go can never be a substitute for putting one foot in front of the other. Discover step by step excitement. To win you must begin.

The first step is the hardest. "That's why many fail—because they don't get started—they don't go. They don't overcome inertia. They don't begin" (W. Clement Stone). Don't be discouraged. Little steps add up, and they add up rapidly.

Dare to begin. No endeavor is worse than that which is not attempted. You don't know what you can do until you have tried. People, like trees, must grow or wither. There's no standing still. Do what you can. "It is always your next move" (N. Hill).

Nugget #95

FEAR IS A POOR CHISEL TO CARVE OUT YOUR TOMORROWS.

The worst liars in the world are your own fears. "Worry is the traitor in our camp that dampens our powder and weakens our aim" (William Jorden).

William Ward showed the difference between faith and worry: "Worry is faith in the negative, trust in the unpleasant, assurance of disaster and belief in defeat . . . Worry is a magnet that attracts negative conditions. Faith is a more powerful force that creates positive circumstances . . . Worry is wasting today's time to clutter up tomorrow's opportunities with yesterday's troubles."

What causes most battles to be lost? It's the unfounded fear of the enemy's strength. A. Purnell Bailey says worry is like a fog: "The Bureau of Standards in Washington tells us that a dense fog covering seven city blocks, one hundred feet deep, is comprised of something less than one glass of water. That amount of water is divided into some 60,000,000 tiny drops. Not much there! Yet when these minute particles settle down over the city or countryside, they can blot out practically all vision. A cup full of worry does just about the same thing. The tiny drops of fretfulness close around our thoughts and we are submerged without vision."

Dale Carnegie wrote, "An old man was asked what had robbed him of joy in his life. His reply was, 'Things that never happened.'" Fear wants you to run from things that aren't after you. It's never safe to look into the future with eyes of fear.

Do you remember the things you were worrying about a year ago? How did they work out? Didn't you waste a lot of energy on account of most of them? Didn't most of them turn out to be all

189.

right after all? Almost 99% of the things that we worry about don't happen.

Here's what I do. I follow this famous advice: "At night, I give all my worries and fears to God. He's going to be up all night anyway." The book of Peter puts it this way: "Let him have all your worries and cares, for he is always thinking about you and watching everything that concerns you."

Never make a decision based on fear. Don't ever find yourself giving something the "benefit of the doubt"—doubt has no benefit. One of the great discoveries you can make is to find that you can do what you were afraid you couldn't do.

Nugget #96

Don't Fly Into A Rage Unless You Are Prepared For A Rough Landing. ◢

A Filipino saying advises, "Postpone today's anger until tomorrow." (Then apply this rule the next day and the next.) When you are upset, take a lesson from modern science: always count down before blasting off. By the way, counting to ten may not be enough; I know sometimes it takes counting to twenty.

Seneca quipped, "The best cure for anger is delay." The book of Proverbs counsels, "He that is slow to anger is better than the mighty; and he that rules his spirit than he that takes a city."

Blowing your stack always adds to the air pollution. How many great ideas have you had while you were angry? How many "expensive words" have you said when you were upset? You'll never get to the top if you keep blowing yours.

Anger is one letter short of danger. People who are constantly blowing fuses are generally left in the dark. If you lose your head, how can you expect to use it?

One of the worst fruits of anger is revenge. No passion of the human heart promises so much and pays so little as that of revenge. The longest odds in the world are those against getting even with someone. Francis Bacon adds, "In taking a revenge a man is but even with his enemies; but in passing it over, he is superior."

Time spent in getting even is better used in trying to get ahead. When trying to get even, you will always do odd things. "Vengeance is a dish that should be eaten cold" (an Old English proverb).

Marcus Antonius reflected, "Consider how much more you often suffer from your anger and grief, than from those very things for which you are angry and grieved." David Hume said, "He is happy whose circumstances suit his temper; but he is more excellent who can suit his temper to any circumstances." Anger is a boomerang that will surely hit you harder than anyone or anything at which you throw it. Keep your temper. No one else wants it.

Nugget #97

GO FARTHER THAN YOU CAN SEE.

Wayne Gretsky is, arguably, the greatest hockey player in history. Asked about his secret for continuing to lead the national hockey league in goals year after year, Gretsky replied, "I skate to where the puck is going to be, not where it has been."

Too many people expect little, ask for little, receive little and are content with little. Having a dream is not trying to believe something regardless of the evidence; dreaming is daring to do something regardless of the consequences. I sincerely believe that every one of us would accomplish many more things if we did not so automatically view them as impossible.

"Don't wait for all the lights to be green before you leave the house" (Jim Stovall). Don't ever say that conditions are not perfect. This will always limit you. If you wait for conditions to be exactly right, you will never do anything.

Those who dare, do; those who dare not, do not. Don't do anything that doesn't require vision. Isak Dineson said, "God made the world round so that we would never be able to see too far down the road." The person who dares for nothing need hope for nothing.

I really believe that the best way to live your life is "outside of the box." The future belongs to those who can think unthinkable thoughts, see where no one is looking and take action before it's obvious.

Let your faith run ahead of your mind. Significant achievements have never been obtained by taking small risks on unimportant issues. "If you're hunting rabbits in tiger country, you must keep your eye peeled for tigers, but when you are hunting tigers you can ignore the rabbits" (Henry Stern). Don't be distracted by the rabbits. Set your sights on "big game."

You have reached stagnation when all you ever exercise is caution. Sometimes you must press ahead despite the pounding fear in your head that says, "Turn back."

Our destiny says to us, "Come to the edge."

We say, "It's too high."

"Come to the edge."

We say, "I might fall."

"Come to the edge," Destiny says.

And we stepped out.

And it pushed us.

And we flew.

THE SECRET TO LIVING IS GIVING.

One way to judge a person is by what they say. A better way is by what they do. The best way is by what they give. Elizabeth Bibesco said, "Blessed are those who can give without remembering and take without forgetting." The big problem is not the haves and have nots–it's the give nots.

Charles Spurgeon said, "Feel for others–in your wallet." An Indian proverb says, "Good people, like clouds, receive only to give away."

The best generosity is that which is quick. When you give quick it is like giving twice. When you give only after being asked you have waited too long.

Whatever good that happens in your life is not so you can keep it all to yourself. Part of it is intended to be given to others. I agree with E.V. Hill when he said, "Whatever God can get through you, He will get to you."

The book of Acts says, "It is more blessed to give than to receive." Giving is always the thermometer of our love for others. Eleanor Roosevelt said, "When you cease to make a contribution, you begin to die." Getters don't get happiness. Givers get it.

When you live for others, it's the best way to live for yourself. There is always room at the top for anyone who is willing to say, "I'll serve." John Wesley advised, "Make all you can, save all you can, give all you can." That's an excellent formula for a successful life.

When it comes to giving, some people stop at nothing. The trouble with too many people who give until it hurts is that they are so sensitive to pain. Greed always diminishes what has been gained. Mike Murdock says, "Giving is proof that you have conquered greed."

If you have, give. If you lack, give. G. D. Bordmen said, "The law of the harvest is to reap more than you sow." It is true: people who give always receive.

Selfishness always ends in self-destruction. John Ruskin hit the nail on the head when he said, "When a man is wrapped up in himself, he makes a pretty small package."

Henry Drummond said, "There is no happiness in having or in getting, but only in giving." The test of generosity is not necessarily how much you give but how much you have left. Henry Thoreau said, "If you give money, spend yourself with it." What you give, lives.

Nugget #99

PESSIMISM NEVER WINS.

Every person has the potential to be passionate. Everyone loves something. We are shaped and motivated by what we love. It reveals our passion. Helen Keller said, "Keep your face to the sunshine and you cannot see the shadow." She showed that enthusiasm is a choice, not a result.

Ignore what you are passionate about, and you ignore one of the greatest potentials inside you. Nothing significant was ever achieved without passion. Follow this success principle found in the book of Ecclesiastes: "Whatever your hand finds to do, do it with all your might."

Most winners are just ex-losers who got passionate. The worst bankruptcy in the world is the person who has lost his enthusiasm, his passion. When you add passion to a belief, it becomes a conviction. Conviction gets more done than belief ever dreamed of.

Driven by passionate conviction, you can do anything you want with your life—except give up on the thing you care about. My friend Mike Murdock said, "What generates passion and zeal in you is a clue to revealing your destiny. What you love is a clue to something you contain."

Life is a passion, or it is nothing. "Without passion man is a mere latent force and a possibility, like the flint which awaits the shock of the iron before it can give forth its spark" (Henri Frederic Ameil).

Passion is the spark for your fuse. In fact, the bigger the challenge or opportunity, the more enthusiasm is required.

Follow this advice for a successful life: "There are many things that will catch my eye, but there are only a very few that catch my heart . . . it is those I consider to pursue" (Tim Redmond).

"GENTLEMEN, WE'RE SURROUNDED BY INSURMOUNTABLE OPPORTUNITIES." (Pogo)

Sometimes as I drive down different parts of the city I live in, I can't help but notice the vast variety of businesses. Many times I pause and think, "That's someone's dream, that's someone's unique idea, that's someone's million-dollar opportunity." I believe there are significant opportunities and ideas around us every day. In fact, "God hides things by putting them near us" (Ralph Waldo Emerson). The best opportunities and ideas are hidden near you. But, you must be on the lookout for them. You can see a thousand opportunities around you every day . . . or nothing. Your big opportunity may be right where you are now.

Too many people spend their whole lives devoted to only solving problems and not recognizing opportunities. Significant growth always comes from building on talents, gifts and strengths and not by solving problems. Where do you hear opportunity knocking? How can you answer that knock? "There are always opportunities everywhere, just as there always have been" (Charles Fillmore).

You can find opportunities close at hand by paying more attention to the things that are working positively in your life than to those that are giving you trouble. Too many times people devote the majority of their effort, time and attention to things that are never going to be productive in their lives. Clear your mind of the things that are out of your control so you can focus and act upon what you can control. One of life's greatest tragedies is to lose an opportunity and not realize it.

"You are, at this moment, standing right in the middle of your own 'acres of diamonds'" (Earl Nightingale). At any moment, you have more possibility than you can act upon. There are million dollar opportunities around you every day.

"The successful person always has a number of projects planned, to which he looks forward. Any one of them could change the course of his life overnight" (Mark Caine). Opportunities? They are all around us. There are opportunities lying dormant everywhere waiting for the observant eye to discover them.

"Wherever there is danger, there lurks opportunity; wherever there is opportunity, there lurks danger. The two are inseparable. They go together" (Earl Nightingale). The stars are constantly shining, but we often do not see them until dark hours. The same is true with opportunities. Problems are opportunities, and there are a lot of th·m around.

Nugget #101

IF THE SHOE FITS, DON'T WEAR IT.

It doesn't happen often, but while I was writing my book, *Let Go of Whatever Makes You Stop*, I was awakened in the middle of the night with this thought, "Don't live within your means."

Even though it was 4:30 a.m., I was so excited about this idea that I awoke my wife and began to "preach" to her about it for several minutes. (She said that the idea was great, but she really needed her sleep.)

What do I mean when I say, "Don't live within your means?" I believe we should act bigger, believe larger and associate higher. Your outlook determines your outcome. So, make your plans BIG.

I'm not encouraging you to go wild, to have no boundaries or be reckless. Certainly we should spend within our means–but not live there. Talk with people smarter than you. Listen to those more insightful than you. Ask questions of those more successful than you. Lend a hand to those less fortunate than you. Don't stay where you are.

I sincerely believe that many people who think they are frugal aren't really frugal. Rather, they are full of fear. The label of frugality, balance or conservativeness is often a mask to cover up a deep-rooted fear in their lives.

Don't make such thorough plans for rainy days that you don't enjoy today's sunshine. Abandon altogether the search for security. "Only the insecure strive for security" (Wayne Dyer).

No matter what the level of your ability, you have been equipped with more potential than you can possibly use in your lifetime. Don't let the future be that time when you wish you'd done what you aren't doing now. You need to have a dream to make a dream come true.

If the shoe fits, don't wear it. If you do, you're not allowing room for growth. Webster knew all about the ineffectiveness of "living within your means." When you look up the word *means* in his dictionary, it tells you to see the word "average." When you decide to live within your means, you are deciding to live an average life.

Do this: know your limits—then ignore them!

About the Author

John Mason is the founder and president of Insight International, an organization dedicated to helping people reach their dreams and fulfill their destiny. He is a popular speaker at numerous churches and conferences throughout the United States and abroad.

He has authored several best-selling books including:

An Enemy Called Average

You're Born An Original—Don't Die A Copy!

Let Go of Whatever Makes You Stop

Conquering An Enemy Called Average

Proverbs Prayers

Ask . . . (Life's Most Important Answers are Found
by Asking the Right Questions)

You can contact him at:

John Mason
P.O. Box 54996
Tulsa, OK 74155